## FIFTY STATE CAPITOLS

MaryAnn —
Here's to open government and peaceful decision-making!
Thanks for the Bonini inspiration for the architecture

— Jim

WWW.FIFTYSTATECAPITOLS.COM

◀ Idaho

# Fifty State Capitols

## The Architecture
## of
## Representative Government

**Jim Stembridge**

Fifty State Capitols: The Architecture of Representative Government
by Jim Stembridge

All photographs by the author

First Edition 2011

10 9 8 7 6 5 4 3 2 1

Copyright © Jim Stembridge, 2011

All Rights reserved. No part of this publication may be reproduced, stored in a retrieval system, or transmitted, in any form or by any means, mechanical, photocopying, recording, or otherwise, without the prior written permission of the copyright owner.

www.fiftystatecapitols.com

Publisher's Cataloging-in-Publication
(Provided by Quality Books, Inc.)

Stembridge, Jim.
    Fifty state capitols : the architecture of
representative government / Jim Stembridge. -- 1st ed.
    p. cm.
    Includes bibliographical references and index.
    LCCN 2010939523
    ISBN-13: 978-0-9830292-0-5
    ISBN-10: 0-9830292-0-2

    1. Capitols. 2. Architecture and state--United States--States. 3. Representative government and representation--United States--States. I. Title.

NA4410.7.S74 2011                  725'.11'0973
                                      QBI10-600217

Design and production by Cohographics, Salem Oregon   www.cohographics.com

Manufactured by Regent Publishing Services, Hong Kong. Printed in China

Published in the U.S.A. by Coho Publishing, Salem, Oregon   www.cohopublishing.com

Cover map image:
Transcontinental Routes, 1918, Library of Congress, Geography and Map Division

# TABLE OF CONTENTS

Introduction: The Architecture of Representative Government    1
Fifty State Capitols (in alphabetical order)    6
Comparing State Capitols    106
Glossary: Architectural Detail and Lexicon    110
Acknowledgments    118
For Further Reference    119
Index of Capitols    121

*Wyoming* ▶

# Introduction: The Architecture of Representative Government

Early in the history of the United States, state capitols were conceived as the home of all state government. As a building type, the state capitol emerged in the late eighteenth century, came of age during the nineteenth, and reached its zenith in the early twentieth, one of the very few purely American architectural forms.

According to Charles Goodsell in *The American Statehouse: Interpreting Democracy's Temples*, the state capitol fostered "a distinct style of politics that mixed colorful leadership, varied partisanship, bicameral opposition, deliberative debate, insider lobbying, uninhibited reporting, bureaucratic growth, and populist activism."

The architects who designed the capitols looked for forms and features symbolic of democracy, finding them most often in ancient Greece and Rome, in the columns, pediments, and porticos of the Parthenon in Athens, the Pantheon in Rome, the Maison Carrée in southern France, and later interpretations, including London's Somerset House (1786) and St. Paul's Cathedral (1710).

Typically housing the three components of state government—legislature, governor, and supreme court—capitols took on a distinctive shape: multi-storied wings housing the two chambers of the legislature, a central rotunda opening up into a dome, with the governor's ceremonial offices often also opening onto the rotunda, and executive suites and court chambers not far down hallways. Visitor galleries overlooking legislative chambers, features first built into the Maryland State House in 1779, are now open to the public in every state capitol. The form and function were set by Maryland, its new dome under construction in 1787 and completed by 1810. Elements common to the ideal American state capitol are a prominent site with manicured grounds; legislative chambers in opposing wings; public galleries with a view of each legislative chamber; a temple-like entrance; and a central dome or tower covering a majestic central space known as the rotunda.

Foremost among the pioneer architects of state capitols was the third president of the United States, the author of the Declaration of Independence, Thomas Jefferson. One of his most famous architectural works (along with the University of Virginia and his home, Monticello) is the capitol of Virginia in Richmond. The building's design was modeled after the Maison Carrée, built at Nîmes in the south of France by the first-century Romans. Virginia's capitol was the first adaptation of a Roman temple to the architecture of American democracy. The building was first occupied in October 1788, the dome completed in 1791.

▲ *Maryland*

With Jefferson, other pioneering architects and master builders set the tone for later capitols. These included Charles Bulfinch, who submitted plans for the Massachusetts capitol (1798) in Boston based on the design of William Chambers's neoclassical Somerset House in London. Bulfinch later designed the Maine capitol and was invited to work on completion of the national Capitol in Washington, D.C. (see p. 120).

The first state capitol to combine the basic elements of dome, rotunda, portico, and balanced wings housing chambers with visitors' galleries was Pennsylvania's, dedicated in 1822 and destroyed by fire in 1897. Prominent later architects include Elijah Myers (Texas, Michigan, and Colorado); Cass Gilbert (Minnesota, West Virginia, and Arkansas); Charles Emlen Bell (Montana, South Dakota); and Charles F. McKim (Alabama, Rhode Island). The oldest capitol still in use representing all elements of the ideal is North Carolina's (1840).

Most states use the term State Capitol to denote the central building housing the governor and legislature. In some states, including Vermont and Maryland, the proper name is State House, and in Ohio, the building is the Statehouse. In the State of Washington, the capitol is a campus of several structures, the most prominent of which is the Legislative Building.

Hardly a state capitol was built without cost overrun, deception, or scandal. In many cases, capitol buildings were constructed (some even donated) to help establish a particular city as the state capital. In Virginia, for example, project directors rushed to construct a foundation on the selected site, Shockoe Hill, before Jefferson's concepts could be fully set to plan, to keep the seat of government from moving back to Williamsburg. The final product, completed in 1798, still resting on its hastily built foundation, barely fit Jefferson's design. In Pennsylvania, the threat of Lancaster was Harrisburg's incentive to get land, capitol, and related buildings secured. Atlanta's capitol was hurried along due to threats to keep the Georgia capitol in Milledgeville.

Plans for state capitols have always been subject to heated discussion and numerous changes among the people who decide funding, namely, state legislators. Beyond cost and function, legislators are largely uninterested in architecture and at best ambivalent when it comes to grandeur. Poor workmanship, inferior materials, imitation finery, and fire hazards often result. *Scagliola*, painted stucco, and brick were often substituted for stone. Heating was often by fireplace. Numerous state capitols burned, necessitating replacement: Kentucky (1824), Alabama (1849), Texas

▲ *Massachussets*

▼ *Pennsylvania*

▼ *Virginia*

*Washington* ▶

(1881), Pennsylvania (1897), North Dakota (1930), Oregon (1935), and others. Brick and stone were advocated as "fireproof" building materials.

When a particularly opulent, ornate public building emerged from the chaos, it was often greeted less than enthusiastically. Critics of Washington's state capitol scheme in Olympia included Rufus Woods, editor of the Wenatchee *Daily World* newspaper. "If the voters of this state could get an opportunity to express themselves regarding this extravagance," Woods editorialized after the unveiling, "they would knock it higher than Halley's Comet. Yea, more. They would come so near removing the state capitol from the city of Olympia that the people of that city would wonder where the lightning struck." Completed in March 1928, Washington's was the last capitol built in the classical style.

No state capitol has been built for thirty years, and only two, Hawaii and New Mexico, in the past eighty years, unless the Arizona (1974) and Florida (1978) office towers are considered. The younger capitols are of the office-tower variety (Nebraska, 1932); simplified art deco style (Oregon, 1937); or both (Louisiana, 1932, and North Dakota, 1935). Alaska is unlikely to get a real capitol in the foreseeable future; costs (both political and financial) appear too high.

▼ *Hawaii*

Few of today's state capitols house all three branches of state government. Supreme courts were ordinarily the first to outgrow the buildings, many moving to nearby buildings of their own. The Louisiana Supreme Court moved 80 miles downriver to New Orleans. Only twelve supreme courts continue to meet in their state capitol buildings: Indiana, Iowa, Kentucky, Minnesota, Nebraska, North Dakota, Oklahoma, Pennsylvania, South Dakota, Utah, West Virginia, and Wisconsin.

In some states, the legislature and governor have left the building as well, leaving just a museum. In Florida, the new office-building capitol is right next door to the old capitol, preserved as the Museum of Florida History. In Arizona, three buildings, housing the governor, house,

▼ *Old Supreme Court Chamber, Nevada*

◄ *Oklahoma*

▼ *Florida*

▼ *Utah*

and senate, respectively, surround the territorial capitol. In North Carolina, government offices, legislative, executive, and judicial, are in nearby buildings, nearly out of sight. In Alabama, where the state constitution requires the legislature to meet in the capitol, the legislature moved out for building renovations, which were completed in 1992; but the legislature has not moved back in and has no plans to do so. Only the governor remains in Alabama's capitol.

Recent capitol renovations and expansions have been especially successful in Texas, Virginia, New Jersey, Utah, and Idaho. New buildings, connected by underground tunnels or protected walkways, greatly increase the efficiency and effectiveness of capitols in Connecticut, Maine, and New Mexico. In a triumph of political will, Oklahoma Governor Frank Keating led the effort to complete that state's capitol dome (dedicated November 16, 2002), nearly a century late, a wonderful addition for Oklahoma, a gem among the nation's capitols. As with many public monuments in the modern age, the names of the private sponsors appear prominently throughout.

State governments provide essential goods and services, not the least of which might be termed "law and order." Under the federal system established by the United States Constitution (Tenth Amendment, 1791), "The powers not delegated to the United States by the Constitution, nor prohibited by it to the States, are reserved to the States respectively, or to the people." Like the national government, states govern through three branches: legislative, executive, and judicial. The legislative branch is charged with passing the state's laws and allocating funds for the running of the government. The responsibility of the executive branch, headed by the governor, is to ensure that state laws are carried out. The judicial branch decides cases that challenge legislation or require interpretation of that legislation. The separation of powers among the three branches allows for a system of checks and balances within government. Each branch has some control over the other two, thus keeping the potential for abuse of power in check.

State government responsibilities include provisions for crime, punishment, and related law enforcement; highways, roads, and other transportation; public education including higher education; business regulation; environmental quality; civil rights; elections; public well-being; the structure of state and local government; a system for the collection of taxes and fees; and appropriations to pay for it all. State governments have been doing all of this continuously, and largely democratically, peacefully, and openly, for more than two centuries, a record difficult to match in the history of civilization.

Numerous state capitols fit the bill as outstanding examples of homes of representative government, containing the actual offices of governor and legislature, the leaders of state government. Among the most ornately and opulently carrying out classical architectural ideals are Minnesota, Pennsylvania, California, Kentucky, Texas, Arkansas, Missouri, West Virginia, New York, Connecticut, Oklahoma, Rhode Island, Illinois, Indiana, Colorado, Utah, South Carolina, Mississippi, Georgia, Kansas, Wisconsin, Michigan, New Jersey, Nebraska, Massachusetts, Louisiana, Washington, Idaho, and Iowa.

Less grandiose, less ornate, more historical, and perhaps more befitting the state image are the capitols of New Hampshire, Vermont, Maine, Oregon, Wyoming, South Dakota, Alaska, Hawaii, Tennessee, Ohio, North Dakota, Delaware, Montana, and New Mexico.

Five state capitols remain as museums, nearly empty of the hustle and bustle of legislative deliberation and executive bureaucracy: Nevada, North Carolina, Arizona, Florida, and Alabama.

The most poignantly historical and influential American state capitols continue to be Maryland and Virginia.

State capitols are among our civilization's best monuments of rep-

▼ *View from the Senate Gallery, Oregon*

▲ *Minnesota*

resentative democracy, where contentious issues amid diverse points of view are resolved, if not calmly, then at least non-violently (for the most part), helping to establish and maintain peace, making possible the pursuit of life, liberty, and happiness among the citizenry.

From its earliest origins as a territory and then a state since 1817, Alabama has had five capital cities, first Saint Stephens, then Cahaba, Huntsville, Tuscaloosa, and, finally, Montgomery.

The 1846 Alabama legislature chose Montgomery, on the Alabama River, as the new state capital from among a number of competing river towns. Andrew Dexter, one of the founders of the town, maintained ownership of prime property, anticipating the capital's eventual move to Montgomery. Dubbed Goat Hill for its use as pasture, the site of the capitol retains the name despite attempts to dignify the spot with names such as Lafayette Hill (after the 1825 visit of the Marquis de Lafayette) and Capitol Hill (after the 1847 construction of the capitol).

In selecting Montgomery, the legislature expressly specified that no public expenditures be made in securing the lands or in erecting the building for the capitol. The citizens of Montgomery rapidly organized, acquired Goat Hill, and erected a building. The new Greek Reviv-

al-style capitol was presented to the state of Alabama on December 6, 1847, but was destroyed by fire just two years later, on December 14, 1849. Moving to temporary quarters, the legislature appropriated $60,000 to construct a new capitol upon the foundations of the burned original. Architect Barachias Holt designed the new structure, also in the Greek Revival style. Additions were made to the original building in 1885 (east wing), 1906 (south wing), 1911 (north wing), and 1992 (east-wing addition).

The rotunda is decorated with a painted masterpiece by Roderick MacKenzie depicting Alabama's history. Alabama's capitol is also known for its distinctive spiral staircase.

The building served as home to the Alabama legislature until 1985, when the legislature moved across the street to a building called the Alabama State House. Officially, the move is "temporary," as the Alabama Constitution requires the legislature to meet in the capitol. A 1984 constitutional amendment allowed the legislature to move to another building if the capitol were to be renovated. Although the renovation was completed in 1992, the legislature has not moved back to the capitol, and has no plans to do so.

The building was known as the Capitol of the Confederacy, and a commemorative marker in the shape of a star on the front steps marks the location where Jefferson Davis stood on February 18, 1861, to take his oath of office as president of the Confederate States of America.

The legendary 1965 Selma-to-Montgomery voting rights march, led by Rev. Martin Luther King, Jr., ended on the street in front of the capitol.

JUNEAU **ALASKA**

On March 30, 1867, Secretary of State William H. Seward signed an agreement with the minister of Russia, ceding possession of the vast territory of Alaska to the United States for the sum of $7.2 million. The agreement was widely referred to as "Seward's Folly" because few could fathom what possible value the 586,000 square miles of wilderness could have.

Following the Klondike gold rush of 1897–98, the U.S. Congress, in April 1912, conferred official territory status upon Alaska. Juneau had replaced Sitka as the capital in 1900, although Juneau is just as isolated as Sitka, unreachable by road in Alaska's southeastern panhandle. The U.S. Congress authorized a capitol building in 1911, U.S. Treasury architects prepared plans, construction began in 1929, and the building opened in 1931. It became state property when Alaska became the forty-ninth state on January 3, 1959.

Construction is brick-faced reinforced concrete. The lower facade is faced with limestone. Limestone and marble used in the four columns of the portico and in the lobby were quarried on Prince of Wales Island in southeast Alaska.

In the lobby, clay-fired sculptures by Joan Bugbee Jackson, *Harvest of the Sea* and *Harvest of the Land* depict hunting and fishing in the 1930s. Other carvings depict principal sources of income for the state: oil and gas, fishing and fish processing, wood products, minerals, tourism, hunting, and trapping. An igloo represents native Alaskans, although they did not live in igloos, preferring sod and driftwood structures called *barabarahs*.

The legislative chambers are on the second floor; the entire third floor is occupied by the Governor and Lieutenant Governor. The Hall of Governors contains pictures of all territorial and state governors.

The building originally contained the post office on the second floor, and when Alaskans were informed that the post office needed to be located on the first floor to provide access from the street, the floors were merely renumbered, with a ramp added to provide access to the post office. The second floor became the first, the former first floor renamed the ground floor.

Because Alaska's capitol, originally designed as an office building, has neither a dome nor a rotunda, Alaska is sometimes said to be the only state without a capitol. Marble and limestone interiors, however, befit a state capitol. In two ballot measures, in 1974 and 1976, the people of Alaska chose Willow, near Anchorage, as their new capital city, but moving costs have proved prohibitive. The idea of a new state capitol building in Juneau lives on.

PHOENIX **ARIZONA**

Beginning in 1863, Arizona's first territorial capital was Prescott. The capital moved to Tucson in 1867, then returned to Prescott in 1877. Moving the capital around was not helping the cause for statehood, so the move to Phoenix in 1889 was final.

The state capitol was built as part of the effort to show that the Arizona Territory was ready for statehood. Ground was broken in 1898, and the building opened in 1900.

The capitol was used by the Constitutional Convention of 1910 that created the state constitution necessary for the state of Arizona to be admitted to the Union. A photograph of the convention's members, posing in front of the building, is on display inside. Not without controversy (the original Congressional resolution was vetoed by President Taft in 1911), Arizona was admitted as the forty-eighth of the United States on February 14, 1912.

The building is made largely from materials indigenous to Arizona, including malapai from Camelback Mountain in the foundation, granite from the Salt River Mountains for the ground floor, tuff stone quarried near Kirkland for the second through fourth floors, and the copper dome. The design is optimized for the desert climate of Arizona, with thick masonry walls that insulate the interior, skylights, and round "bull's-eye" clerestory windows to let heat out of the legislative chambers. The building is topped with a 17-foot-tall wind vane, the *Winged Victory of Samothrace*, visible through the rotunda skylight.

*Winged Victory* has been free to rotate 360 degrees around, except for a time in the 1950s when a group of legislators had her tethered because they were tired of seeing her backside. *Winged Victory's* torch is ninety-two feet above the building's floor.

Underneath *Winged Victory*, the capitol dome, once painted the color of copper, is now real copper.

Arizona's capitol, home to the legislature until 1960 and governor until 1974, remains the symbol of state government, but it is now a museum, surrounded by buildings dating from 1974 that house the actual state government, with the House and Senate each in separate new buildings on either side of the capitol, and executive offices (including the Governor and Secretary of State) in an eight-story State Capitol Executive Tower immediately behind. (In 1957, famed architect Frank Lloyd Wright had submitted a proposal for a new capitol, to be located in nearby Papago Park, but the proposal was rejected.)

# LITTLE ROCK **ARKANSAS**

Construction of the Arkansas capitol took 16 years—from 1899 to 1915. The design was by St. Louis architect George R. Mann. After Mann was fired, accused of bribery in 1909, New York's Cass Gilbert was called in to complete the building. (Gilbert was also involved with the West Virginia and Minnesota capitols.) The exterior is limestone quarried in Batesville, Arkansas. The front entrance doors are 10 feet tall, four inches thick, polished bronze, and were purchased from Tiffany's in New York. The cupola, topping the building at 213 feet, is covered in 24-karat gold leaf.

The gentle hill site was formerly occupied by a prison. The plan was to build the building within the prison walls using convict labor, then tear down the walls and demolish the prison. George Donaghey of Conway, the only professional builder serving on the planning commission, was chosen to lay the foundation. The building's position was determined by eyeball—Donaghey stood on the prison's west wall, sighting down 5th Street to set the center stake. The foundation was laid out on a true north/south axis, but when the prison walls were torn down it was immediately apparent that 5th Street did not run truly east-west, but rather was aligned parallel to the Arkansas River. Considerable landscaping has been done to disguise the nine-degree "error." Donaghey referred to the asymmetry as a lucky accident.

Originally the dome was to be a copy of the dome from Saint Peter's in Rome, but as costs rose, plans started shrinking until finally Donaghey just copied the plans of the elegantly spare dome of the Mississippi capitol. The Arkansas capitol was completed in 1915, whereupon George Donaghey won the governorship on a "completed the capitol" platform.

The interior is constructed of marble from three states—floors and walls from Vermont, columns around the third floor from Colorado, and the grand staircases from Alabama. The dome's interior is 160 feet above the floor. The chandelier is 12 feet in diameter, solid brass, and weighs 4,000 pounds.

At the south end of the third floor, the state's 35 senators meet in the Senate Chamber. At the north end is the House Chamber where the state's 100 representatives meet.

Outside is a memorial—a group of bronze figures—commemorating the "Little Rock Nine," black high school students who attempted to integrate Little Rock's Central High School on September 3, 1957, but were turned away by the Arkansas National Guard under the command of Governor Orval Faubus. Later that month, the nine students enrolled and began attending classes. The sculptures were unveiled in a spirited celebration on August 30, 2005.

In 1850, two years after the discovery of gold at Sutter's Mill, California became the thirty-first state. But California did not have a permanent seat of government until 1860. Several cities competed for the power, prestige, and economic benefit of becoming the new state's capital. Capitol buildings were erected in four other cities (San Jose, Monterey, Vallejo, and Benicia) before Sacramento became the permanent site. Even after Sacramento was chosen in 1854, there were unsuccessful efforts to relocate the capital to Oakland (1858–59), San Jose (1875–78, 1893, and again in 1903), Berkeley (1907), and, finally, back to Monterey (1933–41).

California's capitol has stylistic roots in architecture from democratic antiquity. As designed by architects Reuben Clark and M. F. Butler, the capitol combines Greek Revival and Roman-Corinthian architectural styles, the design tracing back through the national Capitol in Washington, D.C., the Massachusetts statehouse in Boston, the Virginia capitol in Richmond, and the Parthenon, encapsulating the Greek ideals of democracy, beauty, and simplicity.

By 1869, the capitol was partially completed and able to accommodate the legislature and several state officers including the governor. The stately dome was first illuminated by gas lighting on December 16, 1871, and the building was finally complete in 1874.

Its completion came at a high cost for one of its principal architects. In 1864, Reuben Clark was committed to a Stockton mental institution where he died in 1866. According to the hospital's files, the cause of insanity was diagnosed as "continued and close attention to the building of the State Capitol in Sacramento."

California's capitol boasts features found in many state capitols: a portico opening into a central rotunda that rises into a dome, with two wings that extend from the central rotunda. In California's capitol, the Assembly is in the left wing and the Senate is in the right wing.

When the capitol first opened, a Sacramento *Daily Union* reporter described the chambers: "This happy mingling of colors by the painter's brush, this ingenious carving by the skillful worker in wood, that horn of plenty, all tend to impress the mind with pleasurable and patriotic emotions." By the 1970s, all the details described by the reporter had been replaced with white paint, fluorescent lights, and lowered ceilings; architects, historians, structural engineers, and master artisans began six years of renovation and earthquake-protection work in 1975.

> Legislative chambers, the center of any capitol, are usually designed and furnished in grand style. The décor of California's chambers reflects precedents set in the British Parliament. The color red, which dominates the Senate chamber, is from Parliament's House of Lords. In the Assembly Chamber, green predominates, a tradition borrowed from the House of Commons.

Colorado was admitted into the Union on August 1, 1876, becoming the nation's thirty-eighth state. With statehood achieved within a month of the 100th anniversary of the Declaration of Independence, Colorado's nickname is the "Centennial State."

Although Golden had been the official capital for several years, most government business was transacted in Denver, where territorial offices were scattered about town and the legislature met where it could. The new constitution provided that the new state's capital city was to be selected at a general election to be held in 1881; Denver received 30,248 votes, Pueblo 6,047, Colorado Springs 4,790, Canon City 2,788, and Salida 698.

From among twenty-one sets of plans submitted in 1885, "Corinthian" by Elijah E. Myers of Detroit placed first. Myers had designed capitol buildings for Michigan (cornerstone laid February 1872) and Texas (groundbreaking February 1882), but the architect was suddenly dismissed on June 3, 1889, and the Colorado capitol was not completed until 1908, when the dome was leafed with gold and the electric bulb installed on top.

Colorado's capitol is in the Corinthian style, with a Greek-cross floor plan. Its elevation is 5,280 feet above sea level, a mile high. With more accurate measuring, the "mile-high" designation on the capitol's west steps has been moved up three steps (see p. 107). The building was constructed of Colorado materials except for the brass and oak trimmings. Granite was quarried in Gunnison. Interior wainscoting and pillar facings are of Colorado onyx, a rare marble from near Beulah, which features variations in pink, mauve, and maroon coloration. With the supply of Beulah marble exhausted, the basement was finished in white marble. Foundations and walls are Fort Collins sandstone.

The dome is 272 feet tall from grade to light bulb on top. Inside the dome, a narrow, winding passageway of 93 steps leads to an observation deck.

In his proposal for the capitol, Elijah Myers described his design for the central rotunda as follows:

> "The Rotunda is a magnificent feature of the building, and not only adds greatly to its beauty, but is of great utility also in furnishing an abundance of light to the halls and corridors. It has a diameter of forty-five feet, being open from the basement to the diaphragm of the dome, and having balconies surrounding it on a line with several of the floors. The walls of the rotunda are of a proper finish for fresco ornamentation, and will be suitably decorated, and thereby made more attractive and interesting by representations of the men, the industries and resources of the State, all of which have combined to place Colorado in the foremost rank of the sisterhood of States."

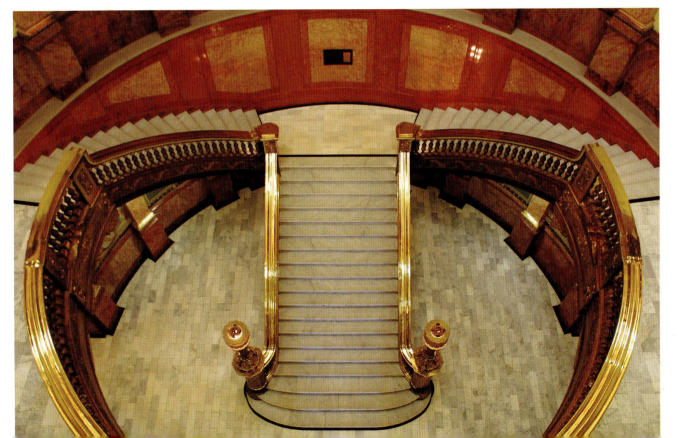

From its earliest days, Connecticut benefitted from a great measure of political independence, proclaiming, in its Fundamental Orders of 1639, the democratic principle of government based on the will of the people. The Fundamental Orders are said to have been the first written constitution of a democratic government—which accounts for Connecticut's nickname, "The Constitution State."

Until the 1880s, Connecticut's capital alternated between New Haven and Hartford. After the capitol building, overlooking Hartford's 41-acre Bushnell Memorial Park, first opened for the General Assembly in January, 1879, the state capitol was in Hartford to stay.

Initial work on the project had begun in 1871, when the legislature established a special commission and appropriated funds. The site was contributed by the City of Hartford, and the commission chose a design by noted architect Richard Michell Upjohn.

The original design called for a modern secular Gothic brick building with a clock tower, in keeping with popular English public architecture of the day. The clock tower concept met with resistance from the commission, which preferred a dome to a tower. Consequently, a re-design made Connecticut's the only state capitol in the High Victorian Gothic style. The dome is a compromise between a traditional Renaissance dome and a traditional English clock tower.

Construction is of marble from East Canaan, Connecticut, and granite from Westerly, Rhode Island. The capitol is crowned by a gilded dome, 54 feet in diameter, rising 257 feet above ground. Interior floors are inlaid with white marble and red slate from Connecticut, plus richly colored Italian marble. During the building's first few years, the marble and brass fountain under the east staircase provided water for legislators' horses tethered to the back porch.

The Senate Chamber configuration has each of 36 senators facing all the others in a large circle. In addition to housing the Senate Chamber, the Hall of the House of Representatives, plus the offices of the Governor, Lieutenant Governor, and Secretary of State, Connecticut's capitol and surrounding grounds abound with images and mementos of state history.

The capitol was designed with 17 tympana (scenes carved from stone) above exterior portals and 26 exterior Gothic niches for sculpture, eight of which remain empty, available for filling in the future (see p. 114). Among the individuals honored with niche sculptures are Roger Sherman—who signed both the Declaration of Independence of 1776 and the Constitution of 1789—and Ella Grasso—state representative, secretary of state, United States congresswoman, and Connecticut governor (1975-80).

Among the tympana, *Putnam Leaving the Plow* depicts Israel Putnam leaving his Connecticut farm to lead Revolutionary War troops at the Battle of Bunker Hill, where he famously said,

"Don't fire until you see the whites of their eyes . . ."

Delaware's Old State House was the first permanent capitol building in Dover. Begun in 1787 and completed by May 1792, this Georgian-style structure was originally home to both state and Kent County governments. Located on the historic Green in Dover, the State House served as a focal point in the state's civic life for over two centuries.

Over the course of 140 years of continuous governmental use, a number of structural and stylistic changes radically altered the original eighteenth-century appearance of the State House. These changes included the addition of wings to accommodate increasing governmental needs, plus the Victorian-style remodeling of the building's exterior in 1873. In 1976, the Old State House was restored to its original eighteenth-century appearance as part of Delaware's bicentennial celebration commemorating the signing of the Declaration of Independence.

The first floor features an 18th-century-style courtroom while the second floor contains the original chambers of the state legislature. The House Chamber contains notable portraits by Thomas Sully of Commodores Jacob Jones and Thomas Macdonough, heroes from the First State who served in the War of 1812. The Senate Chamber houses an imposing portrait of George Washington painted by Denis A. Volozan.

Notable architectural details include the gilt sunflower ceiling sham, and the grand, dual stairways, known as a geometrical staircase, that served as the portal of entry to the legislative chambers. This geometrical staircase was designed by John Howe in 1791. Although Delaware's general assembly now meets in nearby Legislative Hall, the Old State House remains the state's symbolic capitol.

Legislative Hall is a Georgian Revival structure of handmade brick with an 18th-century-style interior. It was designed by architect E. William Martin under the direction of the State Buildings and Grounds Commission created by Governor Buck in 1931. Dedicated in 1933, Legislative Hall provides formal chambers for the Senate and House of Representatives as well as the General Assembly's non-partisan staff agencies. The Governor and Lieutenant Governor also have offices in the building for use while the legislature is in session.

The building was expanded by the addition of north and south wings from 1965 to 1970 to provide legislator offices. Two more wings were added onto the east side of the building in 1994, providing additional office space for legislators and their staffs as well as hearing and caucus rooms. Legislative Hall was renovated in three phases during the summers of 1995, 1996, and 1997.

O ver the years, Florida's capital cities have reflected the growth of the state. In the early 1820s, legislators transferred government business from St. Augustine to Pensacola for alternating sessions. Travel was hazardous and took almost twenty days—clearly an unsatisfactory arrangement. Tallahassee, halfway between St. Augustine and Pensacola, was chosen as the capital of American Florida in 1824.

Florida became the twenty-seventh of the United States on March 3, 1845, and the brick capitol was completed that same year. Both the front and rear porticos were dignified with six Doric columns, which are thirteen feet in circumference and thirty-four feet in height.

In 1891, the capitol was repainted, a small cupola added, and plumbing installed. The first major alteration came in 1902 with the addition of two wings and the dome, which to many Floridians symbolizes their government. The dome is covered with a dark copper, which has oxidized to a soft patina. Both the east and west facades have a bas-relief of the state seal in their pediments (see p. 115). Further additions to the capitol were made in 1923, 1936, and 1947.

The early twentieth century was the last time all branches of Florida's government operated under one roof. State government offices began moving to other buildings in 1911. Following intense debates about moving the capital to Orlando, the legislature, in 1972, authorized money for a new Tallahassee capitol complex to include house and senate chambers, along with a 22-story executive office building. The structures were completed in 1977.

Florida's capitol complex now includes the executive tower west of the old capitol, plus domed house and senate chambers to the north and south, with legislative office structures adjacent to each. The executive tower's top is 300 feet above the ground floor; only the capitols of Louisiana, Nebraska, Illinois, and Texas are taller. The building was officially dedicated on March 31, 1978. *Stormsong*, a sculpture of playful dolphins in the Florida Heritage Fountain fronting the capitol, dates from 2003.

Artist James Rosenquist created *Images of the Sunshine State*, two murals in the plaza level of the executive tower, symbolizing Florida industry and recreation, including exploration of outer space and playing at the beach. Legislative chambers provide ample space for desks, computer connections, camera coverage, and electronic voting equipment for Florida's 40 senators and 120 representatives. Private passageways keep legislators separated from the public.

After it had been vacated in 1978, the old capitol was refurbished to its 1902 image. Today, it serves as the Museum of Florida History, with special exhibits, artifacts, and reproductions displayed in the halls, meeting rooms, Governor's suite, Supreme Court, and legislative chambers.

A classic Renaissance design by the architectural firm of Edbrooke and Burnham of Chicago, the building follows architectural precedents established by the United States Capitol. Oolitic limestone from Indiana is the chief building material. Georgia marble was used for the interior walls, floors, and steps, as well as the cornerstone. Every effort was made to obtain material, including wood and iron, from Georgia. A formal dedication ceremony was held July 4, 1889.

The rotunda extends from the second floor up 237 feet into the dome. The gilded dome, measuring 75 feet in diameter, rises to a total height of 272 feet. The dome was originally covered with an alloy of lead and tin. The cupola is topped with a 15-foot-tall female statue, *Miss Freedom*, holding a torch in one hand and a sword in the other. At night, *Miss Freedom's* torch is lit.

The capitol originally consisted of three main stories with a basement used as a stable. During the first major renovation project, in 1929, the basement was converted to offices and the floors renumbered. The basement is now the first floor with the main entrance on the second floor.

The capitol currently houses the offices of the Governor, Lieutenant Governor, and Secretary of State. Also within the capitol are chambers for the state's Senate and House of Representatives, house and senate offices, and committee meeting rooms. The highly decorative legislative chambers are on the third floor—House of Representatives to the west and Senate to the east. The desks in the red-carpeted House are of hand-carved cherry wood, while the blue-carpeted Senate has carved oak desks.

In earlier years, an observation room atop the capitol dome was popular with residents of Atlanta and visitors, offering a panoramic vista of the city and views of both Stone Mountain and Kennesaw Mountain. For safety reasons, it is now closed to the public.

Georgia, the last of the 13 original British colonies, was founded by James Edward Oglethorpe on February 12, 1733, at the present site of the city of Savannah, as a refuge for Englishmen who could not pay their debts.

Savannah, Augusta, Louisville, and Milledgeville have served as the center of Georgia's government. Milledgeville was Georgia's capital city for sixty years. On December 5, 1877, however, the voters of Georgia chose Atlanta as the capital. Capitol construction began on November 13, 1884, on the site of the old Atlanta city hall, and the cornerstone was laid on September 2, 1885.

# HONOLULU
# HAWAII

> The Capitol's airy, open style suits it ideally to the gentle Hawaiian climate. Here is a Capitol where the sun, rain, and tradewinds are free to enter. The great central court, open to the sun and rain, moon and stars, rises to the sky like the throat of one of the volcanoes that helped build this land.
>
> Symbolism of the Capitol
> Office of the Governor

Hawaii's capitol is designed to resemble a volcano, specifically, Punchbowl on the island of Oahu, within sight of the building, and many of its design features are symbolic. The capitol is surrounded by a reflecting pond, representing the Pacific Ocean. The 40 pillars supporting the roof symbolize coconut palms, a major source of food, water, and building materials for Hawaiians, one of the most useful trees in the world. The support pillars on the top floor are grouped in eights, to represent the eight Hawaiian islands: Hawai'i, Kaho'olawe, Kaua'i, Lana'i, Moloka'i, Ni'ihau, O'ahu, and Maui.

The capitol, in downtown Honolulu, opened March 15, 1969; a renovation was completed in 1995.

Entrances to the building are on the *mauka* (toward the mountains) and *makai* (toward the sea) sides of the building. A statue of Queen Liliuokalani is on the *makia* (ocean) side, which faces `Iolani Palace, and one of Father Damien (Saint Damien of Molokai, the Catholic priest who ministered to lepers on the island of Molokai) is on the *mauka* side, which faces Punchbowl. Bronze replicas of the state seal, each 15 feet in diameter and weighing 7,500 pounds, hang from the capitol's *mauka* and *makai* entrances. There are no doors to the grand entryways, only open spaces to welcome the wind and bid it "aloha" as it makes its way from the mountains toward the sea.

The main courtyard is open to the sky, an anti-dome symbolizing openness. In the center of the courtyard is the mosaic *Aquarius*, designed by Maui artist Tadashi Sato, made up of 6 million tiny tiles imported from Italy. The mosaic depicts the changing colors and patterns of the sea surrounding Hawaii. From the courtyard, doors lead into public galleries overlooking each legislative chamber. The Governor's Office welcomes visitors on the top floor.

BOISE **IDAHO**

**B**oise was the Idaho territorial capital in 1865 and became the state capital when Idaho was admitted to statehood in 1890.

Construction of the present capitol started in 1905. The central section, including the dome, was completed in 1912. Designed by J.E. Tourtellotte and Charles Hummel, it is a standard neoclassic style, patterned after the United States Capitol. Construction of wings was completed in 1920. The site of the building enhances its authoritative scale. Including the dome with its gilded 5 foot 7 inch solid copper eagle on top, it is 208 feet high.

The dome is topped with a traditional illuminated lantern—a perch for the eagle, which serves as a symbol of both Idaho's aspirations as a state and its allegiance to the larger democracy. The outside walls are faced with sandstone from state-owned Table Rock east of Boise. Convict labor was used to quarry and deliver the sandstone blocks, some weighing ten tons. The sandstone blocks on the first floor were cut to evoke the walls of a log cabin.

Inside the capitol, large pillars of steel covered with a veneer of *scagliola* (a mixture of granite, marble dust, gypsum, and glue, dyed to look like marble) rise in the rotunda to the dome (see p. 117). The *scagliola* veneer was created by a family of artisans from Italy. In 1976, it was repaired by injecting marble dust and glue into the cracks with hypodermic needles. The surface was then covered with a polyurethane finish to protect it.

The corridors, floors, wainscoting, and base throughout the building consist of 50,646 square feet of artistically carved marble. There are four kinds blended into the interior: green swirled Vermont marble on the walls, gray Alaska marble with inlaid patterns of near black in the floors, Italian marble in four grand staircases, and reddish pink Georgia marble in the trim.

In the rotunda, thirteen large stars represent the thirteen original colonies, and forty-three smaller stars symbolize Idaho's entry into the Union as the forty-third state. A marble compass rose centers on a sundial constructed of minerals found in Idaho, symbolizing the state's great abundance of natural resources.

Idaho's is the only capitol building in the United States heated by geothermal water. A pumping station provides enough hot water to heat 750,000 square feet of building space on all but the most severe winter days. The 3,000-foot well can produce about 1,000 gallons per minute of water at 165 degrees F. under natural artesian pressure. The system was first used in the winter of 1982–83.

Illinois was admitted to the Union as the twenty-first state on December 3, 1818. Since that date, Illinois has been governed from three different cities and from six capitol buildings.

Kaskaskia, fifty miles south of St. Louis, was the seat of the territorial government and became the first Illinois state capital. Vandalia was the second. Influenced by a local Springfield lawyer and state legislator named Abraham Lincoln, the 1833 General Assembly empowered voters to decide the location of the new capital city, and they chose Springfield, sixty miles north of Vandalia. Abraham Lincoln was in the original capitol in Springfield frequently as both lawyer and politician, serving in the House of Representatives and delivering the famous 1858 "House Divided" speech in Representatives Hall. The building was also the scene of President Lincoln's lying-in-state, on the 3rd and 4th of May, 1865.

A new capitol building, the state's sixth, was built on a site known as the Mather Block, the highest point of ground in Springfield. Many in the city had wished the site to be used as the burial place of Abraham Lincoln. Mrs. Lincoln, however, preferred Oak Ridge Cemetery, a mile north. So, with President Lincoln interred at Oak Ridge, ground was broken on March 11, 1868, for the new capitol.

The building was designed by Chicago architect John C. Cochrane in the shape of a Greek cross. Due to lack of funding, construction halted in 1877. It resumed in 1884 and the building was completed in 1888. The outer walls are limestone from Joliet and Lemont, Illinois; porticos are granite; and staircases, columns, and floors are domestic and imported marble. *Carton-pierre*, a type of paper maché, was used for much of the ornamentation. The skyscraper-style capitols of Louisiana and Nebraska are taller overall, but the Illinois capitol dome is the tallest of all state capitol domes. From the first floor, it is 361 feet to the top of the dome and 405 feet to the top of the flagpole. The 92-foot-diameter rotunda is encircled above corbel statues by a plaster frieze, the work of local artist T. Nicolai. The frieze, considered by many to be the best artwork in the capitol, is painted to resemble bronze.

At the top of the rotunda is a seal of the State of Illinois made of 9,000 pieces of stained glass.

- Were it not for the Great Chicago Fire of October 8–9, 1871, Chicago might have become the capital of Illinois. The legislature had planned to meet in Chicago that fall, but stayed in Springfield instead.

- Abraham Lincoln's home is several blocks east of the current capitol, preserved for public viewing. The previous capitol building, so often used by Lincoln while he was in Springfield, is several blocks to the north.

INDIANAPOLIS **INDIANA**

In 1825, after nine years of statehood, Indiana's capital moved from Corydon to Indianapolis, only four years after Alexander Ralston laid out the new town. State Treasurer Samuel Merrill transported state documents and the treasury from Corydon to the new capital city in wagons. That trip, which takes about three hours to drive today, took Merrill ten days over rough roads and trails.

Indiana is the Hoosier State, its citizens known as Hoosiers, though no one knows exactly why.

Planning for Indiana's current statehouse began in 1867 and the building was completed in 1888. The design of Edwin May, an Indianapolis architect, was selected. Shaped like a Greek cross, the structure features a central dome and rotunda. The main floor, fourteen feet above ground level, holds the governor's offices. On the second floor, May placed the chamber for the House of Representatives on the east, balanced by the Senate chamber on the west. Offices and other rooms surrounded the open atriums, and the Indiana Supreme Court was located in the north end.

The interior was designed in the style of the Italian Renaissance. Whenever possible, the plan called for Indiana materials. For instance, wainscoting, doors, and trim are Indiana oak, maple, and walnut. Atrium skylights brighten the north and south wings. The central feature of the rotunda is a striking art glass inner dome, primarily in blue tones, suspended below a skylight. The stained glass rotunda window is made from German glass.

The exterior is Corinthian in design. Here too the architect called for Indiana materials. The walls are brick, covered with oolitic limestone quarried from Monroe, Lawrence, and Owen counties. The foundation of blue limestone comes from Greensburg and North Vernon.

The year the building was completed, 1888, Indiana was thrust into the national spotlight with the election of Indianapolis attorney Benjamin Harrison as president of the United States.

The capitol has its share of mysteries, including rumors of ghosts haunting its halls. Treasures have been unearthed, including an old brass cannon found in the basement in 1905 and seven bars of silver found locked in an old safe in 1995.

Indiana is one of the few states in the nation that continue to operate all three branches of government out of its original capitol. The historic building is filled with the faint echoes of voices locked in political debate over wars, taxes, women's rights, and civil rights. Citizen legislators have passed laws here, governors have led their implementation from here, and judges have ruled here on their constitutionality, decisions that have affected every Hoosier's life.

The Iowa capitol in Des Moines, built between 1871 and 1886, is one of the nation's finest examples of nineteenth-century architecture. It is the third capitol for Iowa, the second in Des Moines. Renovations were completed in 1983. Its most commanding feature is the towering 80-foot diameter dome, 275 feet above the ground floor, constructed of steel and brick, gilded with 23-karat gold leaf (one of ten gold-domed capitols). On top of the dome is a belvedere, and on top of the belvedere, a golden lantern (see p. 111). Four smaller golden lanterns top copper-covered domes at the four corners of the building. The five domes make the building unique and easily recognizable among American state capitols.

Inside, the building features 29 types and colors of marble, plus works of art, fixtures, and carvings in both wood and stone.

The building was dedicated in January 1884, when the General Assembly first met in its new chambers.

After fifteen years of construction, an audit showed $3.77 unaccounted for. The interior, however, remained unfinished until decorative artist Elmer E. Garnsey of New York completed his work on the vaulted ceilings, halls, corridors, and dome interior in the early 1900s.

He wrote:

"It would seem that the strongly-colored marbles and granite of wainscot and columns demand a color scheme of sober richness . . . The most important consideration of such a scheme is that it should be considered as a whole; that the character and use of the building, as the visible heart and brain of the state, receive constant consideration . . ."

The interior of the dome appears to be trimmed in gold leaf, but the substance is actually aluminum leaf with shellac. Some 240 light bulbs illuminate it.

Above the rotunda are twelve gilded bronze statues representing *History, Science, Law, Fame, Literature, Industry, Peace, Commerce, Agriculture, Victory, Truth*, and *Progress*.

Tile floors, intricate iron grillwork, and gracefully spiraling staircases highlight the large law library directly above the main entrance. The library contains the accumulated laws and court decisions from Iowa, other states, and the federal government.

Outside on the capitol grounds are several sculptures, including *Lincoln and Tad*, sculpted by Fred and Mabel Torey of Des Moines, dedicated on the anniversary of the Gettysburg Address, November 19, 1961.

Most of present-day Kansas came to the United States as part of the Louisiana Purchase in 1803. When Kansas became a territory, on May 30, 1854, federal law specified that the citizens of the new territory should decide the issue of slavery for themselves.

Settlers poured in, with pro- and anti-slavery groups vying to pack the state with sympathizers. In the 1855 elections, pro-slavery candidates won control of the legislature and violence broke out, led by fanatic abolitionist John Brown. The pro-slavery group wrote a constitution favoring slavery, but Kansas voters rejected it. Anti-slavery citizens then wrote a new constitution forbidding slavery and Kansas voters approved. At this moment in the nation's history, several Southern states seceded, and the question of Kansas statehood was a bone of contention in the United States Congress. Kansas was admitted to the Union as the nation's thirty-fourth state on January 29, 1861. The following November, voters chose Topeka as the state's capital. The style selected for the new capitol was Italian Renaissance Revival, which symbolized democracy in the language of nineteenth-century public architecture. It was built in sections. The cornerstone of the east wing was laid October 17, 1866. The foundation was originally brown sandstone, quar-

ried from the bluffs along Deer Creek in Shawnee County. But the soft stone deteriorated quickly, and the foundation had to be torn out and rebuilt in limestone. That section of the building was finished in 1873. Work began on the west wing in 1879 and it was occupied in 1880. The central section with its towering dome was authorized in 1881, work began in 1885, and all structural work on the capitol was finished by 1903.

The Kansas capitol measures 304 feet from the ground to the top of the cupola. The copper dome is 66 feet in diameter.. The legislative chambers are richly decorated with marble from a wide variety of sources. In the Senate Chamber, the round windows on each side, imported from France, are a combination of faceted and stained glass, designed to accentuate the rays of the sun. John Steuart Curry's famous mural *Tragic Prelude* in the east wing expresses the fury of "bloody Kansas," the prelude to the Civil War, and the painful infancy of the State of Kansas. In the outstretched left hand of the gigantic figure of John Brown is the Word of God, and in his right hand a "Beecher bible"—better known as a rifle. Flanking him, facing each other, are contending free soil and pro-slavery forces, and at their feet, two figures symbolic of the 1.5 million Civil War dead and wounded. In the background are pioneers with their wagons on the endless trek west, a tornado, and a raging prairie fire.

# FRANKFORT KENTUCKY

In May 1769, Daniel Boone passed through the Cumberland Gap into the Kentucky country, exploring as far west as present-day Louisville. Six years later, he oversaw clearing of the Wilderness Road. Soon after, delegates from such pioneer settlements as Ford Harrod and Boiling Springs met at the commonwealth's first "capitol"—a stately elm tree. On June 1, 1792, the Commonwealth of Kentucky entered the Union as the fifteenth state.

Kentucky's fourth and current capitol building in Frankfort, Neoclassic Revival in style, was dedicated June 2, 1910, following a long and bitter quarrel among Louisville, Lexington, and Frankfort over which city should be the state's capital. Part of the building's cost was paid with federal funds, reparations over damages caused by Union soldiers during the Civil War. Because the design was too immense for the old public square downtown, the present site in south Frankfort was chosen. The many striking architectural features and opulent decorative finishes in Kentucky's capitol illustrate architect Frank Mills's penchant for classical French interiors and the Beaux-Arts style.

The interior is elegant. Massive marble stairways at each end of the building were patterned after those in the Paris Opera. Walls and staircases are white Georgia marble; the floors of light Tennessee marble and black Italian marble. On axis with the rotunda, the grand corridors feature 36 imposing columns of Vermont granite and delicate art glass skylights.

In the soaring rotunda, at the exact center of the building, stands a larger-than-life statue of Abraham Lincoln, surrounded by four sculptures of prominent Kentuckians, including Jefferson Davis and Henry Clay. Lincoln was born in Kentucky, near Hodgenville. Tradition holds that touching Lincoln's boot brings good luck.

The French influence extends to the State Reception Room, inspired by Marie Antoinette's drawing room in the Palace of Versailles. Mirrors flanking either end of the room reflect the chandeliers, creating a hall-of-mirrors effect. Designed for ceremonial events, the room is decorated with pilasters finished in *scagliola* as well as murals painted to resemble Gobelin tapestry.

Decorative lunettes above each staircase highlight the entrances to the House and Senate chambers. Painted in oils by T. Gilbert White, both depict frontier scenes with Daniel Boone.

The exterior, faced in Indiana limestone and Vermont granite, boasts four porticos created by seventy Ionic columns, each 28 feet high. The richly sculptured pediment of the classical front portico was designed by Charles Henry Niehaus and carved by Australian sculptor Peter Rossack. Allegorical figures represent Kentucky, the central female figure, with *Progress, History, Plenty, Law, Art*, and *Labor* as her attendants.

In addition to being the seat of government for the state, the Louisiana capitol in Baton Rouge is a memorial to Huey P. Long, former Governor and former United States Senator from Louisiana. As governor, Long worked hard to convince the public and the legislature that a new capitol was needed. He stood in the back of the room as legislators changed their votes to approve the project, in special session, early in the Great Depression. The new building was dedicated on May 16, 1932, and became the scene of Huey Long's assassination in September 1935 at the age of 42.

Of art deco design, the 34-story building stands 450 feet tall, the tallest state capitol in the United States. It is one of four skyscraper capitols (North Dakota, Arizona, and Florida are the others) and one of nine state capitols without a dome.

A grandiose set of stairs lead to the main entrance. The forty-nine steps contain the names of the fifty states in order of their admission to the Union. The last step lists both Alaska and Hawaii. Louisiana's state symbol, the pelican, decorates the sides of the staircase.

Immediately inside, Memorial Hall, measuring 35 by 120 feet and two stories high, is the central public space of the building. The floor is made of Mt. Vesuvius lava from Italy. Four marble statues show likenesses of prominent Louisianans, including P. B. S. Pinchback, Louisiana's only black governor. Murals painted by French artist Jules Guerin depict Louisiana as a land of plenty.

The House Chamber walls are of Crazannes Anteor marble from France with panels of Siena travertine from Italy. The ceiling is of Celotex, which is made from bagasse, a byproduct of sugar cane refining. Four bronze chandeliers weighing one ton each are on pulleys so that they can be easily lowered and raised.

The Senate Chamber walls and columns are of Famosa Violet from Germany and Brocatelle Violet from France. The floor is Roman travertine. The ceiling consists of 64 hexagonal tiles, one for each parish in Louisiana. The ceiling is scarred near the main entrance as the result of a 1970 bomb explosion. Luckily, the bomb detonated on a Sunday afternoon and no one was injured, although only two of four original columns survived.

Louisiana's capitol grounds, among the most beautiful in the nation, can be viewed from the capitol's observation deck high above. The 27 acres contain an abundance of native Louisiana plants and trees, including oaks, magnolias, and azaleas. The focal point is the statue of Huey P. Long, erected in 1940, because the capitol was his dream. Buried under the statue is Huey P. Long himself.

**M**aine separated from Massachusetts, becoming its own state in 1820. Portland, Brunswick, Hallowell, Waterville, Belfast, Wiscasset, and Augusta each sought the honor of becoming the state capital. Augusta won when Governor Enoch Lincoln signed the state legislature's designation bill on February 24, 1827.

Maine's statehouse and grounds sit on thirty-four acres along the banks of the Kennebec River, the first capitol park in the nation. Architect Charles Bulfinch of Boston designed the building. In original form, it resembles his design for the Massachusetts statehouse, which had been the capitol for Maine's citizens before the creation of the state of Maine. After Bulfinch saw the park setting, he increased the size of the cupola for better scale.

The cornerstone was laid on July 4th, 1829, amid impressive Masonic ceremonies. Construction was of granite from Hallowell quarries, with painted wood interiors. The Maine legislature held its first session in the new state capitol on January 4, 1832.

The interior of the capitol was remodeled in 1852 and again in 1860. A three-story wing was added to the rear in 1890–1891. Major remodeling completed in 1910 established the present-day appearance of the building, including the addition of a dome, rising to a height of 185 feet, built to replace the original cupola. Topping the dome is a statue, the draped female figure of *Wisdom*, designed by W. Clark Noble of Gardiner, made of copper overlaid with gold leaf. A more recent renovation includes a greatly improved sky-lit passage to the adjoining Cross Office Building.

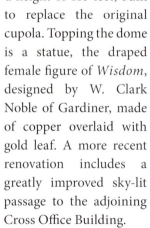

The House of Representatives occupies the third and fourth floors of the north wing of the capitol; the Senate Chambers occupy similar quarters in the south wing. On the second floor, along with the Hall of Flags and the Law Library, the Governor's office overlooks the adjoining State Office Building.

Throughout the capitol are portraits of governors and other outstanding men and women of Maine. The Senate Chamber art collection includes portraits of Abraham Lincoln and Maine's Hannibal Hamlin, Lincoln's first vice president. The Hall of Flags features white Doric columns, old battle flags, and governors' busts.

Black limestone floor tiles contain a variety of marine invertebrate fossils. Fossiliferous limestone was first installed during construction of the west wing during 1889 and 1890. Additional fossil-bearing limestone was installed during the extensive remodeling and renovation from 1909 to 1911. The composition and fossil content of the stone is consistent with the carbonaceous limestone of the Middle Ordovician Crown Point Formation at Isle La Motte on Lake Champlain, Vermont, which is its most likely source. Near the center of the floor under the rotunda is a swirl-shaped fossil, one of several that are more than 475 million years old.

# ANNAPOLIS
# MARYLAND

The Maryland State House is the nation's oldest capitol still in legislative use. On March 28, 1772, Governor Robert Eden laid the cornerstone on State Circle in Annapolis. When the Continental Congress came to Annapolis to meet in the old Senate Chamber in November 1783, Maryland's capitol became the only statehouse ever to serve as the nation's capitol. But the Continental Congress found the State House unfinished and leaky.

On December 23, 1783, General George Washington came before Congress to resign his commission as Commander-in-Chief of the Continental Army, an event captured in famous paintings by John Trumbull (1824) and Edwin White (1859). Setting the tone for the nation's founding, Washington left immediately after the ceremony to return to Mount Vernon and private life as a farmer. A bronze plaque on the floor marks the spot where he stood to deliver his farewell speech.

By the summer of 1788, the exterior of the new dome was completed. It was constructed of timber supplied by the Dashiell family of Somerset County, and no nails were used. The dome is still held together by wooden pegs reinforced by iron straps. The height of the interior, from floor to ceiling, is 113 feet. The exterior height is 181 feet. Thomas Jefferson and James Madison are said to have spent three hours on the balcony of the dome in September 1790 enjoying the view of Annapolis houses from their perch above town.

The interior of the original statehouse is wood and plaster. The Colonial Revival addition, dating from 1906, has matched veined Italian marble walls and columns. A broad black line across the lobby marks the border between the two sections. The skylight in the House of Delegates Chamber is by Tiffany & Co. The Italian marble on the walls is an unusual rust and black, colors reminiscent of the gold and black Maryland state flag.

The new Senate Chamber has four large paintings of Maryland's signers of the Declaration of Independence, including Charles Carroll of Carrollton, painted by Thomas Sully. At the time of his death in 1832, Carroll was the last surviving signer.

As if to reinforce the historic significance of Maryland's capitol, above the landing of the main staircase is Edwin White's 1859 painting *Washington Resigning His Commission*. There he is, the familiar George Washington, addressing the Continental Congress in the old Senate Chamber a few steps away.

In 1713, the seat of Massachusetts government was the Old State House at King (now Washington) and State streets in Boston. After the American Revolution, leaders of the new state wanted a larger, more elegant home. They selected a site close to the south-side summit of Beacon Hill, overlooking Boston Common and the Back Bay—once John Hancock's cow pasture. Designed by native-born architect Charles Bulfinch, the new State House was completed on January 11, 1798. Paul Revere

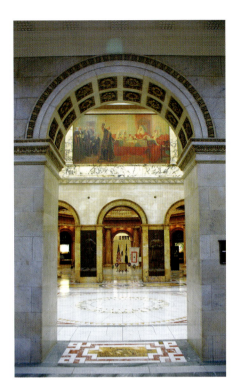

and Sons coppered the dome in 1802 to prevent water leakage, and seventy years later the dome was gilded with gold leaf. The "Bulfinch Front," as it is called, faces south, its red bricks, white trim, and golden dome catching the sun in every season.

Between 1889 and 1895, a large extension, built of yellow brick, was added to the back of the Bulfinch State House, its interior making extensive use of marble, wrought iron, and carved wood paneling. White-marble wings to the east and west were added in 1917.

Inside, Doric Hall has served as the reception room for uncounted banquets, news conferences, swearing-in ceremonies, and other special events. Doric Hall derives its name from the architectural style of its ten columns. The next room, Nurses' Hall, features murals by Robert Reid depicting events crucial to the start of the American Revolution, including the Boston Tea Party of December 16, 1773, and Paul Revere's ride of April 19, 1775. The high-domed ceiling of the central room, Memorial Hall, appears to be under the State House dome, but it is not. Farther back into the building, beyond the Grand Staircase, is the Great Hall, completed in 1990 and used for official state functions and receptions. Lining the hall are 351 flags representing the cities and towns of Massachusetts.

Directly below the gold dome is the Senate Chamber. Busts of Presidents Washington and Lincoln are behind the rostrum. Nearby is a bust of the Marquis de Lafayette, who visited the chamber on his way to lay the cornerstone of the Bunker Hill Monument in 1825.

The House Chamber, paneled in Honduras mahogany, is in the State House's 1895 rear addition. Above the public galleries is the famous Sacred Cod, symbolizing the importance of the fishing industry in the early Massachusetts economy, given to the House of Representatives by Boston merchant Jonathan Rowe in 1784.

On the grounds outside and below the capitol are statues of orator Daniel Webster, educator Horace Mann, religious martyr Mary Dyer, and the thirty-fifth president of the United States, John F. Kennedy.

In 1837, Michigan was admitted to the Union. The state constitution provided that Detroit would be the capital until 1847, when the legislature would decide on a permanent location. In 1847, with Ann Arbor, Jackson, and Marshall in contention, the legislature named Lansing as the new state capital. Although opponents termed Lansing a "howling wilderness," a temporary capitol building was erected, and by 1871 a new capitol was in the works.

Michigan's was the first of several state capitols to be designed by Elijah E. Myers during the 1870s and 1880s. (Others were Texas, Colorado, Idaho, and Utah.)

Construction began in 1872. The millions of bricks for walls and ceilings were made locally, but the stone for the facade came from Ohio, the cast iron for the dome and floor beams from Pennsylvania, and the marble for the floors from Vermont. The building was dedicated on January 1, 1879. A restoration was completed in 1992.

The building's style, incorporating motifs from classical Greek and Roman architecture, is variously termed Renaissance Revival or neoclassical. Columns in the classical orders—Doric, Ionic, and Corinthian—are found both outside and inside the building. A four-story central pavilion is flanked by the balanced wings of the House and Senate. Above the building is a graceful cast-iron dome, its finial 267 feet above ground level.

In the center of the building is the glass-floored rotunda. The glass floor is made up of 976 pieces of glass, each about five-eighths of an inch thick. The floor, 44½ feet in diameter, creates an optical illusion: seen from above it appears to be a bowl. Walls are solid brick and—except for the rotunda's glass floor—even the ceilings and floors are brick.

The rotunda rises 160 feet to the top of the inner dome. The oculus or eye in the top of the dome provides a glimpse into the vastness of the universe, represented by a starry sky.

The entrance hall is adorned with faux marble columns, pilasters, and wainscot. The columns are cast iron, the pilasters are plaster, and the wainscot is pine, all hand painted

to imitate the opulence of the Victorian age. The results are masterpieces of craftsmanship rather than merely a showcase of expensive materials.

Twenty chandeliers light the capitol's main corridors. Originally lit by gas, they are ornamented with an elk and shield from the state's coat-of-arms. Doorknobs also feature Michigan's coat-of-arms.

SAINT PAUL MINNESOTA

On January 2, 1905, thousands of Minnesotans streamed through the richly decorated halls and chambers at the opening of their new state capitol. The building is the third to serve as Minnesota's seat of government. The first was built in 1853 in downtown St. Paul. The second, in 1883, also at the downtown site, was thought cramped and stuffy. So in 1895, more than 40 designs for a new capitol for Minnesota were entered in competition. The winning design was the work of influential local architect Cass Gilbert, who later designed the Arkansas capitol and helped finish the West Virginia capitol. Gilbert insisted on using dazzling white Georgia marble for the upper walls and dome—one of the Minnesota capitol's most brilliant features. He called for Minnesota-quarried granites and sandstones for the lower levels, steps, and terraces, and local Kasota stone for much of the interior. The stone used in the ground floor exterior is granite from St. Cloud.

Gilbert's design is dominated by its dome, consciously reminiscent of the U.S. Capitol in Washington, D.C., and the Basilica of St. Peter in Rome. Like St. Peter's, it has stone ribs, deeply pierced windows on its surface, and a drum with pairs of columns separated by window openings. The dome's peak is 223 feet above ground.

At the base of the dome is a gleaming gold sculpture designed by Daniel Chester French and Edward Potter—a four-horse chariot and figures—officially known as *Progress of the State* but usually referred to as the "Quadriga." The four horses represent the power of nature: earth, wind, fire, and water. The women symbolize civilization, and the man standing in the chariot represents prosperity. Below the Quadriga are six colossal figures representing the *Virtues*, sculpted in white marble, also designed by French. Twelve stone eagles stand guard around the dome, and the exterior is further enlivened by classical wreaths, plaques, and other carvings.

An inner dome of brick and steel supports the exterior marble of the dome. Under the dome, in the center of the rotunda is a large star, symbol of Minnesota, the North Star State. A crystal chandelier six feet in diameter hangs over the rotunda.

The second floor is the "grand floor," with three chambers—House, Senate, and Supreme Court. The Senate Chamber is in the west wing, the House in back, the Supreme Court in the east wing. On the ground floor, the Rathskeller Cafeteria is reminiscent of a German dining hall.

Mississippi is named for the Mississippi River, which forms its western boundary. Roughly translated from Native American folklore, the name means "Father of Waters." Mississippi was admitted as the twentieth state on December 10, 1817. The capital city, Jackson, is Mississippi's largest metropolitan area.

The Mississippi state capitol, the third one built in Jackson, was completed in 1903. The building was designed by St. Louis architect Theodore Link and erected on the site of the old state penitentiary. The building's cost was paid with back taxes owed by the Illinois Central Railroad. A restoration was completed in 1983.

The Beaux-Arts-style capitol is a grandiose symmetrical design filled with classical detail. It houses the legislative and executive branches of Mississippi state government. (The judicial branch moved to the Gartin Justice Building across High Street.)

The eagle atop the 180-foot-high dome is solid copper coated with gold leaf, eight feet high and fifteen feet wide. Inside the dome, the rotunda contains 750 light bulbs illuminating the relief medallion *Blind Justice* and scenes representing Mississippi history: Indians, a Spanish explorer, and a Confederate general. Legislative wings terminate in semi-circular Corinthian colonnades topped with sky-lighted saucer domes over the house and senate chambers. In all, some 4,750 bulbs brighten the building's interior.

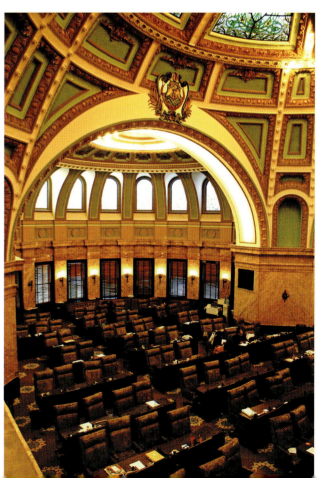

On the first floor, the Hall of Governors displays portraits of Mississippi's governors since the creation of the Mississippi territory in 1798. The old State Library and the Supreme Court chambers, now committee meeting rooms, are on the second floor. On the third floor are found the Legislature, Governor, and Lieutenant Governor. Public views of both chambers, from the galleries, are on the fourth floor.

The grounds of Mississippi's capitol, right out front, feature a statue memorializing the women—mothers, sisters, wives, and daughters—of the Confederacy. Among the trees is the state tree, the magnolia.

JEFFERSON CITY
MISSOURI

Missouri, part of President Thomas Jefferson's 1803 Louisiana Purchase, became a state after the 1820 Missouri Compromise allowed Missouri to enter the Union as a slave state and Maine to enter the Union as a free state, thus keeping the balance of slave states and free states equal in Congress.

Missouri was admitted as the twenty-fourth state on August 10, 1821. St. Charles was the state capital until Jefferson City was designated as the permanent location. The present capitol building was completed in 1917 and stands on the same spot as its predecessor, high atop a bluff overlooking the Missouri River.

The structure, covering nearly three acres, is a symmetrical building of the Roman Renaissance style, surmounted by a dome. It stands on 285 concrete piers which extend to solid rock at depths from 20 to 50 feet. The exterior is of limestone marble from Carthage, Missouri, as are the corridor floors, rotundas, and stairway treads.

The grand stairway is 30 feet wide, among the widest stairways in the world, and extends from the front portico to the third floor. It is more than 65 feet from the wall on one side of the stairway to the wall on the other side. At the entrance is a mammoth bronze front door, 13 feet by 18 feet.

Atop the lantern of the capitol dome, 260 feet above the ground, is a classic bronze figure of Ceres, the Roman goddess of grain, chosen to symbolize the state's agricultural heritage.

A 13-foot bronze statue of Thomas Jefferson, the creation of sculptor James Earle Fraser, graces the entrance of the capitol. Inside, the view up into the dome from the first floor rotunda includes a bronze chandelier, weighing 9,000 pounds, hanging from the dome's eye 171 feet above. Artwork throughout the building depicts dramatic scenes of Missouri's history, countryside, and people. Especially famous are murals by artist Thomas Hart Benton in the lounge of the House of Representatives. In December of 1936, Benton finished what may be his best known work, *The Social History of the State of Missouri*, including representations of Jesse James, Huckleberry Finn, the Pony Express, the Civil War, and many other people, places, and events that helped shape Missouri into what it is today.

Missouri is the "Show Me" state. The slogan, while not official, is common throughout the state and is used on Missouri license plates. Legend attributes the phrase to Missouri Congressman Willard Duncan Vandiver, who, speaking at an 1899 naval banquet in Philadelphia, declared, "I come from a state that raises corn and cotton and cockleburs and Democrats, and frothy eloquence neither convinces nor satisfies me. I am from Missouri. You have got to show me."

**M**ontana became a state on November 8, 1889. Legislators—unwilling to risk the political consequences of deciding themselves—let the people choose the new state's capital city. An 1892 referendum led to a vitriolic runoff two years later between the two top contenders, Helena and Anaconda. Helena, backed by Butte Copper King (and future Senator) William A. Clark, narrowly defeated Anaconda, Marcus Daly's company town. The victory, according to "Queen City" supporters, delivered the state from the stranglehold of Marcus Daly and his Anaconda Copper Mine.

On a gentle slope surrounded by 10 acres of spacious lawns, Montana's capitol looks north over Prickly Pear Valley. The cornerstone was laid in 1899 and the building was dedicated in 1902. The two wing additions were

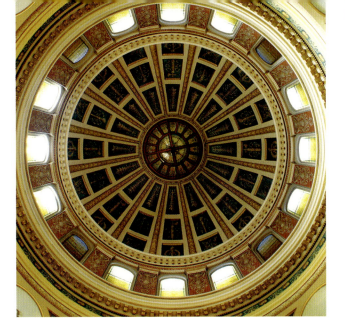

completed in 1912. In the 1960s, a major renovation expanded and restored the capitol to its original appearance. The building is constructed of sandstone and granite. A statue, *Liberty*, stands atop the copper dome.

Inside, the centerpiece of the 1960s restoration is the barrel-vault ceiling, its arched skylight made of 90 stained-glass windows held in place by red-oak frames. Statues of former United States Congress leader Mike Mansfield and his wife Maureen Mansfield occupy prominent places on the third-floor south balcony. The many paintings in the capitol include—behind the Speaker's desk in the House Chamber—Charles M. Russell's 1912 depiction of Lewis and Clark meeting the Flathead Indians at Ross Hole near Missoula on September 5, 1805 (see p. 109). The historic painting is oil on canvas, 12 feet by 25 feet. Amedee Joullin's painting *Driving of the Golden Spike* (at what is now Brigham City, Utah), a gift from the Northern Pacific Railroad, is installed inside the arch at the end of the barrel vault.

Montana's capitol is unusual in that the House and Senate chambers are in the same wing; when new House chambers were constructed in the 1912 west wing, the Senate moved into the old House chamber, also on the building's west side. On the east are the old Senate cham-

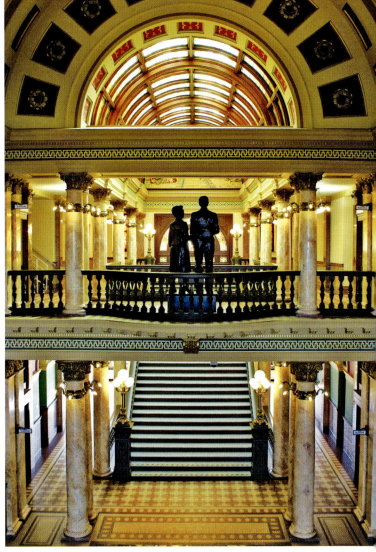

ber, also used for a time by the Montana Supreme Court, and the Governor's offices.

The Gallery of Outstanding Montanans was established by the state's legislature in 1979 to pay homage to citizens of the Treasure State who made significant contributions to their fields while epitomizing the unique spirit and character of Montana. Honorees rotate into the gallery, each honored for an eight-year period. The gallery includes artist Charles M. Russell, newscaster Chet Huntley, actor Gary Cooper, and statesman Mike Mansfield.

LINCOLN NEBRASKA

In response to westward migration and the call for a transcontinental railroad, President Franklin Pierce signed the Kansas-Nebraska Act on May 30, 1854, creating the Nebraska Territory. After statehood, March 1, 1867 (the thirty-seventh state), the legislature voted to move the state capital from Omaha to the small community of Lancaster, south of the Platte River and along the western edge of settlement in the new state. The new capital city, which was also to be home to Nebraska's university, penitentiary, and state hospital, was renamed Lincoln.

The Nebraska's state capitol (its third) is the nation's first statehouse design to depart radically from the prototypical form of the national Capitol. New York architect Bertram Grosvenor Goodhue won the nationwide design competition with his "Tower on the Plains." Four states have since followed Nebraska in building office towers: North Dakota, Florida, Louisiana, and Arizona. Nebraska's capitol, with furnishings and landscaping, was constructed in four phases over ten years, from 1922 to 1932.

Clad with Indiana limestone, the building has a low, wide base in the plan of a cross within a square, creating four interior courtyards. From the center of the base rises a 400-foot tower, topped by a dome, and crowned with the 19-foot-tall bronze figure *The Sower*. A thematic progression of 23 exterior stone carvings,

beginning above the north entrance, represents events in the 3,000-year history of democracy as a form of government. The ornamental interior features numerous marble-columned chambers with vaulted polychrome tile ceilings (see p. 117), marble mosaic floors, and murals depicting the history of Nebraska's Native American and pioneer cultures.

The rotunda, 112 feet tall, is located at the intersection of the arms of the cross in the center of the building. The theme of the rotunda is "Virtues of the State." Three large murals painted by Kenneth Evett date from 1956: *The Labors of the Hand* represents industry, *The Labors of the Head* represents intellect, and *The Labors of the Heart* represents humanitarian works.

In the east and west arms of the central cross are the two chambers built for Nebraska's legislature. Nebraska had a bicameral government until the Unicameral, a single legislative body, was formed in 1937. The west chamber was chosen to house the new body because it was larger. The chambers are decorated to represent the two groups who brought their cultures into the Plains. The east chamber

symbolizes the aboriginal life of the Indian. The west chamber symbolizes the European age of settlement, with the successive appearance of the Spanish, French, and Anglo-American upon Nebraska soil.

# CARSON CITY NEVADA

When the ambitious founders of Carson City laid out the town in 1858, they had dreams of a new territory, with a new state to follow. Ten acres, known as the Plaza, were set aside in the belief that Carson City would be chosen as the capital of a new government in western Utah Territory.

The Nevada Territory was created by Congress in 1861 and the territorial legislature selected the fledging community of Carson City as its capital, but the Plaza remained empty, even after Nevada became the thirty-sixth state to join the Union, in 1864. Carson City was named the capital, but the constitutional convention determined that no state capitol would be built until after three legislative sessions. Some hoped that the capital would be moved to a more central location, but that did not happen.

San Francisco architect Joseph Gosling designed the Nevada capitol, and local building contractor Peter Cavanaugh did the construction between 1870 and 1871. It is a two-story masonry Classical Revival structure that incorporates Renaissance Revival and Italianate elements. To keep costs low, sandstone was obtained free of charge from the Nevada State Prison quarry, just outside Carson City. The original footprint of the capitol was cruciform, a central rectangle with two wings. The first floor contained a major office at each corner connected by central halls. The wings of the second floor were built for the two legislative chambers—the Assembly and the Senate. The octagonal dome topped with a cupola admitted light to the second story. In 1906, an octagonal annex was added to the rear (east) of the building to house the state library.

By the early twentieth century, the legislature had outgrown the building, so Nevada architect Frederic DeLongchamps was contracted to design northern and southern legislative wings. Completed in 1915, the wings use stone from the same quarry as the original capitol.

Nevada's capitol was the tallest building in Carson City until the Ormsby House casino was erected in 1972. Legend depicts the capitol dome's cupola as made of silver. In actuality, it was first constructed of tin and then, after a retrofit, of silver-colored fiberglass.

For more than 50 years, all three branches of state government were housed in the capitol. The Nevada Supreme Court met here until 1937, when it moved into an adjacent building. The state legislature met here until 1971, when it moved to its new Legislative Building south of the capitol. All Nevada governors except the first have had their office headquarters in the capitol. Today, the capitol continues to serve the Governor, and contains historical exhibits on the second floor.

New Hampshire is one of the original 13 colonies. The state's capital city, then called Penacook, was first settled in 1727. The town's name was changed to Rumford in 1733, then to Concord in 1765. In 1808, New Hampshire moved its capital there from Portsmouth, after consideration of Portsmouth, Salisbury, and Hopkinton. A short time later, the capitol was built. Considerable expense was saved by using local granite and by having prison inmates do the cutting, shaping, and facing of the stones.

The final feature, a huge wooden eagle, gold-painted, was raised to the top of the dome in 1818, with the toast "The American Eagle—may the shadow of his wings protect every acre of our united continent and the lightning of his eye flash terror and defeat through the ranks of our enemies." The first legislative session in the new building was held in 1819. New Hampshire's capitol remains the oldest statehouse in the nation in which the legislature continues to meet in its original chambers. Capitols in Massachusetts, Virginia, and Maryland are older, but their legislatures have moved to newer chambers. Vermont claims to have the oldest legislative chambers in their original condition.

The New Hampshire capitol features a double-portico entrance, Doric columns supporting Corinthian columns, topped by a classic Roman triangular pediment. Its dome is relatively small when compared with other capitols, more of a cupola than a dome, and not so much a part of the building as placed on top of the building. Nevertheless, it is an elegant symbol of representative government. The eagle, on its perch since 1818, is 118 feet above the ground.

New Hampshire's legislators continue to meet in their original rooms: 24 senators in the Senate Chamber and 400 members of the House of Representatives—the most of any state—in Representatives Hall, which looks more like a theater than a legislative chamber. Five portraits

are the principle features of the room: the subjects are John P. Hale, Abraham Lincoln, George Washington, Franklin Pierce, and Daniel Webster. The capitol also houses the Governor's and Secretary of State's offices and meeting space for the five-member Executive Council.

Crumbling antique banners of New Hampshire history are on display in the capitol's front room, known as the Hall of Flags. Out front, the most prominent statuary is of New Hampshire-born Daniel Webster (1782–1852), eloquent orator and United States Secretary of State under three presidents, and Franklin Pierce (1804–1869), fourteenth president of the United States, the only U.S. president from New Hampshire.

# TRENTON NEW JERSEY

The original New Jersey State House was built in 1792 by Jonathan Doane, not long after New Jersey ratified the Constitution, thus becoming the third state in the newly created United States. Two provinces known as East and West Jersey each had its own capital, Perth Amboy in the east and Burlington in the west. The newly unified legislature voted to establish Trenton as the permanent capital, and construction of the State House began.

The new capitol was two and a half stories high with seven bays radiating off a center hall and a bell-tower in the center of the roof. Legislative chambers were on the first floor: Senate (then called the Legislative Council) on the west and General Assembly on the east. The Governor's and judicial offices occupied the second floor.

Over the past two centuries, New Jersey's capitol has expanded many times, but parts of the original building are still in use as the Governor's private chambers, making New Jersey's capitol the second oldest in continuous use.

An office wing on the north side was added in 1845, with a two-story portico, pairs of Corinthian col-

umns, and a classical pediment. The new entrance was a two-story porch with six fluted Doric columns. A grand rotunda, capped by a spherical dome and cupola, connected the old and new wings. New wings for both legislative chambers were added in 1871, with the old Senate chamber modified to accommodate the Governor's office. More additions and remodeling followed a fire in 1885.

Thomas Edison's Electric Light Company (of New Jersey) installed the 66-bulb brass chandelier in the new Assembly Chamber in 1891, new technology at the time. Wall sconces were piped for old-fashioned gas light, just in case the new technology failed.

The original east wing was replaced with a four-story office section in 1906. The most recent major renovation, completed in 1999, included refurbishing the golden dome and interior rotunda space, restoring the legislative portion of the building, and adding legislative office space, known as the South Addition, a pedestrian tunnel, and a multi-level parking garage.

Today, the Assembly Chamber boasts stained-glass lunettes and an enormous skylight. Gold leafing from 1898 decorates ornamental plaster work. A brightly painted wooden statue depicting the great seal of the State of New Jersey stands atop a high arch over the Speaker's dais. Carpeting incorporates images of four state symbols: purple violet, eastern goldfinch, red oak, and honey bee.

In the Senate Chamber, sixteen symbolic murals celebrate New Jersey's hard-won freedom and prosperity. Scenes include the Revolutionary War battles of Trenton, Princeton, and Monmouth.

A sculpture honors Woodrow Wilson, professor (1890–1902) and president (1902–1910) of Princeton University, governor (1911–1912) of New Jersey, and president (1913–1920) of the United States.

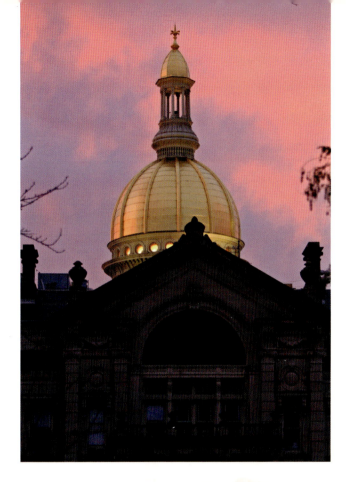

SANTA FE
NEW MEXICO

New Mexico has the oldest as well as one of the newest capitols in the United States. The oldest is the Palace of the Governors on the Plaza in Santa Fe, completed in 1610. The oldest public building in the United States, it served as the region's capitol for colonial Spain, Mexico, the Pueblo Indians, and the Confederacy (for a couple of weeks in 1862). The 400-year-old building is now a museum.

On January 6, 1912, President William Howard Taft signed the proclamation admitting New Mexico as the forty-seventh state. A three-story, silver-domed territorial capitol building, completed in 1900, served as the state capitol for fifty years. Its dome removed, it is now known as the Bataan Memorial Building.

New Mexico's new capitol, a blend of New Mexico territorial style and Pueblo Indian adobe architecture with Greek Revival adaptations, was dedicated on December 8, 1966. Unique among state capitols, it is round, with entrance courts on four sides. Seen from above, it is in the shape of a Zia, the Indian sun symbol—a circle radiating in four directions (see p. 109). In each direction, four straight lines of varying length personify the number most often used by "the Giver of all good gifts," including:

- the earth, and its four directions;
- the year, and its four seasons;
- the day, with sunrise, noon, evening, and night;
- life, with its four divisions—childhood, youth, adulthood, and old age; and
- humans, with their four sacred obligations: to develop strong bodies, clear minds, and pure spirits, along with devotion to the welfare of people.

The Zia also appears on the state flag, making New Mexico the only state that displays a diagram of its capitol on its flag.

The capitol's interior design and decoration represent the state well. A shallow (60 feet high), skylight-lit, three-story rotunda (49 feet in diameter) is in the center, with spacious Senate and House chambers on opposite sides, public viewing galleries, and bands of offices along the outside walls, including the Governor's Office on the top floor. The capitol's many connecting radial and circumferential corridors are rich in New Mexican art—historic art, Native art, and contemporary art, including contemporary interpretations of historic and Native art.

Under the capitol's surrounding walkways, hidden from view, is parking. A lovely, long, decorated and skylighted walkway connects the capitol with a staff office building, which also boasts galleries of art works as well as a small rotunda.

Santa Fe's historic central Plaza and the 400-year-old Palace of the Governors are five blocks north.

ALBANY NEW YORK

After 32 years of construction, the New York state capitol was completed in 1899. British architect Thomas Fuller had started work on the building in 1867. Eight years later, Fuller was replaced by two American architects, Leopold Eidlitz and Henry Hobson Richardson, resulting in an unusual blend of Italian Renaissance, French Renaissance, and Romanesque features. The capitol is constructed principally of gray granite. Foundation walls are more than sixteen feet thick. It is one of ten state capitols without domes.

The single largest room in the capitol is the Assembly Chamber, its massive volume created by a 56-foot-high vaulted sandstone ceiling, painted in bands of greenish-blue, red, and black, highlighted with gold. Supporting the spectacular groined arches are four pillars of polished granite. The Assembly Chamber ceiling began to crumble, however, as the building settled. After a large rock fell, a new ceiling was installed four feet below the original, hiding the crowning elements of the original room, two large murals by William Morris Hunt.

The most prominent interior features of New York's capitol are its three staircases of carved stone bathed in skylight. The Great Western Staircase, also known as the "Million Dollar Staircase"—119 feet high, with a 3,000-square-foot skylight at the top—took 14 years to construct. Among the famous faces carved into the sandstone are George Washington, Abraham Lincoln, Thomas Jefferson, Alexander Hamilton, Benjamin Franklin, Susan B. Anthony, and Clara Barton.

The Senate staircase is red Corsehill sandstone from Scotland. Corsehill sandstone is soft when first quarried, allowing stone carvers to work easily. The stone then hardens slowly with continuing exposure to air. Carved creatures gain in complexity as the stairs progress upwards, embodying the theme of evolution, at the time a recently discovered concept.

First occupied in 1881, the Senate Chamber has a richly carved golden oak ceiling with deeply paneled recesses that create an acoustically perfect "debate arena." At the back of the chamber are two large fireplaces. Designed as sources of heat, they now serve as quiet meeting areas for senators to walk into and discuss the issues of the day privately—"fireplace chats" away from the chamber.

The large desk in the Executive Chamber has been used by every governor since 1881. When wheelchair-bound Franklin Delano Roosevelt became governor of New York in 1929, he wanted a way to get from the garage to this office without using public elevators. A hidden door was cut in the paneling so Governor Roosevelt could use a nearby service elevator. When closed, the door blends perfectly with the paneled wall.

During much of the Colonial period, North Carolina was without a fixed capital. Governors lived in their own homes and the Assembly moved from place to place, meeting in private homes or courthouses. Edenton (1722) and New Bern (1766) were capitals before 1788, when a state convention fixed the capital in Wake County, and a plan for Raleigh was drawn up. The present building, its cornerstone laid in 1833, was completed in 1840.

Although it is a fine example of Greek Revival architecture, North Carolina's capitol today is merely a symbol of state government. The Supreme Court moved out in 1888, and the General Assembly moved two blocks north to the State Legislative Building in 1963, the first of five state legislatures to move to its own building (Arizona, Nevada, Florida, and Alabama have followed). The historical North Carolina capitol, now a museum, is the site of occasional hearings, meetings, and "photo opportunities." It is perhaps the least changed of any civic building of its era.

In plan, the capitol is a cross shape, centering on a domed rotunda,

which measures 97 feet from the floor to the crown atop the dome. The building is small, just 160 feet by 140 feet. The east and west "fronts" are identical; over the years, the east facade has come to be recognized as the front. Exterior walls are gneiss, a form of granite, quarried nearby. Interior walls are stone and brick. Massive wooden trusses bear the weight of the roof. The capitol's elegantly maintained small park, six-acre Union Square, is filled with trees, making the building difficult to view in its entirety.

Most of the architectural details—moldings, ornamental plaster, and the honeysuckle crown atop the dome—were patterned after ancient Greek temples. Exterior Doric columns are modeled on those of the Parthenon in Athens. The House of Representatives Chamber follows the semi-circular plan of a Greek theater and its architectural ornamentation is in the Corinthian style of the Tower of Winds in Athens. The Senate Chamber is decorated in the Ionic style of the Erechtheum, also in Athens.

At the center of the rotunda is a copy of Italian artist Antonio Canova's unusual sculpture of George Washington (the 1820 original was destroyed when the capitol burned in 1831). Never having seen Washington, Canova depicts him as a seated, contemplative Roman general, complete with tunic and cape (see p. 109).

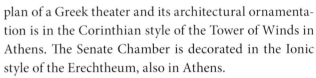

The capitol grounds feature a number of sculptures, including a monument to the three presidents of the United States with North Carolinian roots, Andrew Jackson, James Knox Polk, and Andrew Johnson, and a memorial to North Carolinians' heroism in defeat during the Civil War.

# Bismarck
# North Dakota

When North Dakota became a state, November 2, 1889, Bismarck was its capital. North Dakota was the thirty-ninth (or perhaps the fortieth) state, admitted on the same day as South Dakota. On December 28, 1930, fire destroyed the state's first capitol building, so plans were begun to build a replacement. Construction on the new North Dakota capitol was delayed for a time because construction workers demanded that their pay be raised to 50 cents an hour (up from 30 cents). The Governor called in the state's National Guard to quell a small riot, and the building was completed and first occupied in January 1935.

The 19-story, 241-feet-high building, art deco in style, is the home of North Dakota's legislature and executive-branch agencies, including the Governor's office. The only state capitol that is obviously not symmetrical, with legislative functions to one side and executive functions on the other, it is said to be especially efficient in space and operation.

The main ceremonial space, just inside the main front doors, is Memorial Hall, with a ceiling 40 feet above its Tennessee marble floors. Elevator doors and revolving entry doors include bronze figures symbolizing the history and industry of North Dakota. The lobby walls are Yellowstone travertine from Montana, and the columns and window frames are bronze. On the eighteenth floor is a public observation deck. The building is faced with Wisconsin black granite and white Indiana limestone.

The building's art deco styling is perhaps best recognized in Legislative Hall, between the two chambers, where low glass fixtures in curly maple panels illuminate long benches in rosewood cubicles. The House Chamber walls are American chestnut; the Senate Chamber walls are quarter-sawn English oak. Downstairs is the Theodore Roosevelt Roughriders Gallery, where prominent North Dakotans, including Roger Maris, Peggy Lee, and Lawrence Welk, are honored.

The 130-acre grounds include an especially poignant statue of Sakakawea, the Shoshone Indian who helped guide Lewis and Clark's explorations of the Louisiana Purchase, with her infant son Pomp. Lewis and Clark's party stayed the winter of 1805 along the Missouri River at Fort Mandan, a few miles from the present-day capital of North Dakota.

# COLUMBUS **OHIO**

In Ohio's early history, Chillicothe and Zanesville took turns as state capitals, but Columbus has been the state capital since 1816.

The Ohio Statehouse is the eighth-oldest working capitol in the nation. Construction began with a ceremonial laying of the cornerstone July 4, 1839. The building opened in 1857 when legislators began meeting in their respective chambers and most executive offices were occupied. When fully completed in 1861, it was the nation's largest capitol. It is a masonry structure in the Greek Revival style, largely of Columbus-area limestone. The foundation stone goes more than 18 feet deep.

Spanning 120 feet from the floor to the skylight, the rotunda distributes light to other areas of the building. In the center of the colorful skylight, 29 feet in diameter, is the Seal of Ohio. The rotunda floor is made from nearly 5,000 pieces of hand-cut marble from around the world: salmon stones from Portugal, black and green marble from Vermont, and white marble from Italy. The floor design is symbolic of U.S. history to 1860.

Indoor plumbing was an innovation when the Ohio statehouse was built. Since women were not a part of the legislative process at the time, women's restrooms were not included. In 1876, more restrooms were added near the House Chamber, but the sewer vents were accidentally connected to the building's ventilation ducts, and for the next eight years, the air in the Statehouse was unpleasantly odoriferous.

The Senate Chamber accommodates Ohio's 33 senators. The décor features some 25 colors of paint. Columns in the rear of the room are white Pennsylvania marble topped with Corinthian capitals. Public galleries line both sides on the floor level. The marble dais was carved on site from a piece of marble so massive that it had to be in the room before the walls and ceilings were built. The suspended pedestal on the wall behind the dais is an example of *trompe l'oeil* painting, appearing to be three-dimensional.

On the other side of the rotunda, the House Chamber accommodates Ohio's 99 elected state representatives. The ornate, cantilevered side balconies were part of the original design. A third balcony, the so-called Ladies Gallery, was added at the rear of the House Chamber in 1891.

In front of the capitol, the McKinley monument was erected in 1906 to honor William

McKinley, former Ohio governor and U.S. president, who was assassinated in 1901. Ohio has provided the nation with seven other presidents: Ulysses S. Grant, Warren G. Harding, William Howard Taft, Benjamin Harrison, William Henry Harrison, Rutherford B. Hayes, and James Garfield.

OKLAHOMA CITY **OKLAHOMA**

In the early 1800s, under intense pressure to remove Indians from the eastern states, the U.S. government reserved Oklahoma for Native Americans and, in 1828, required all settlers to leave the area. Between 1830 and 1842, the "five civilized tribes"—Chickasaw, Choctaw, Seminole, Creek, and Cherokee—were compelled to give up their homelands and move to Oklahoma. The Cherokee people refer to this migration as the Trail of Tears. Soon, however, settlers and railroads coveted the reserved Indian Territory, so it was divided into two parts, and, at noon on April 22, 1889, the western half was opened for settlement and established as Oklahoma Territory. (Settlers who entered early, illegally, were known as "Sooners.") Demands for Indian land continued, and a commission was formed to negotiate with the tribes for their land and to dissolve the Indian nations. At the direction of Congress, a new constitution combined Indian Territory and Oklahoma Territory into one new state, and Oklahoma was admitted as the forty-sixth state on November 16, 1907.

All three branches of Oklahoma state government are in its capitol. The building, neoclassical in style, combines elements from ancient Greece and Rome. It is built primarily of Indiana limestone, with pink and black granites quarried in Oklahoma. Most of the flooring is Alabama marble, and much of the trim is Vermont marble. For nearly a century, however, the capitol was without a dome. Construction money had run out before

the dome could be built, so the building was "finished" in 1917 without it. The dome was finally completed and dedicated on November 16, 2002, the nation's newest state capitol dome. Inside the rotunda and up into the dome, everything above a purple ring is new. Renovation work in 1993 and 1999 restored original ceilings, skylights, and other features.

The capitol is rich with more than 100 works of art. In the rotunda, four bright murals by Charles Banks Wilson highlight Oklahoma history—*Discovery and Exploration, Frontier Trade, Indian Immigration, and Non-Indian Settlement*, which tells the story of forced land sales and the state's legendary land runs of 1889 and 1893. Rotunda portraits include famous Oklahomans Will Rogers, Woody Guthrie, Wiley Post, and Jim Thorpe.

On the second floor are the Blue Room, used by the governor for official ceremonies; the Supreme Court Chambers; and a replica of the 22-foot-9-inch sculpture atop the capitol dome, *The Guardian*, representing all Native American cultures.

On the floor of the rotunda, in the Great Seal of the State of Oklahoma, five rays represent the Five Civilized Tribes.

The Oklahoma capitol is surrounded by working oil wells. The well across from the entrance is nicknamed "Petunia #1" because the drilling began in the middle of a flower bed (see p. 109).

In the spring of 1843, early settlers in the Oregon Territory gathered for a "wolf meeting" to discuss the destruction of livestock by wild animals. On May 2, at Champoeg, by a vote of 52-50, those wanting the beginnings of government in Oregon prevailed. The historic scene is depicted in a mural by Barry Falkner behind the Speaker's rostrum inside Oregon's capitol, in Salem.

When Oregon was admitted as the Union's thirty-third state, on February 14, 1859, it took several weeks for word to cross the country, the news reaching Oregon on March 17. Behind the Senate President's rostrum, a mural by Frank H. Schwarz commemorates arrival of the news. Oregon continues to celebrate two birthdays, February 14 and March 17.

Following destruction of the previous building by fire, a new Oregon capitol was designed by New York architect Francis Keally in the Modern Greek style. Dedicated October 1, 1938, its exterior is white marble from Danby, Vermont, while its interior is largely rose travertine from Montana. Floors and staircases are Phoenix Napoleon grey marble from Missouri and black Vermont marble. Wings added in 1967, containing offices for Oregon legislators (60 representatives and 30 senators), were remodeled in 2008.

In the center of the rotunda floor is the state seal, cast in bronze. Surrounding the rotunda are murals illustrating significant events in the state's early history: Captain Robert Gray crossing the bar at the mouth of the Columbia River, 1792; Lewis and Clark's expedition, 1805; the first women to cross the continent to Oregon, 1836; and the first wagon train to Oregon, 1843. Rising above, to a height of 106 feet, is the interior of the dome. The ceiling's 33 stars symbolize Oregon as the thirty-third state.

Sweeping staircases lead up from the rotunda to the House and Senate chambers on the second floor (see p. 116). Also on the second floor are the governor's offices, behind a balcony that provides a unique theatrical setting for public ceremonies.

The House Chamber is fashioned of bright golden oak, the Senate Chamber of somber black walnut. Carpeting in the legislative chambers features the three most important commodities of Oregon's early economy, the state tree, Douglas fir, in the House, salmon and wheat in the Senate.

Outside, Oregon's unique flat-top dome rises 140 feet above ground, topped by the gilded *Oregon Pioneer*,

who adds another 23 feet. The dome's deck, reached by a climb of 121 steps, provides a sweeping view of Salem.

Massive marble relief sculptures by Leo Friedlander, depicting a covered-wagon family on the Oregon Trail and the Lewis and Clark Expedition's arrival, flank the entrance to the capitol, with maps of the respective routes carved on the backs.

# HARRISBURG PENNSYLVANIA

The earliest Pennsylvania statehouse, dating from 1735, was in Philadelphia. Now known as Independence Hall, it was where the Declaration of Independence and the Constitution of the United States were debated and signed. Beginning in 1790, Philadelphia was the nation's capital, and the state and national legislatures both met in the building. In 1799, the Pennsylvania State Assembly moved west to Lancaster, and a year later the United States Congress moved to Washington, D.C.

The legislature moved from Lancaster to Harrisburg in 1812, and a capitol building was dedicated on January 2, 1822. After the first capitol burned during a snowstorm in 1897, Philadelphia architect Joseph M. Huston won the right to finish the partially built replacement. He chose the Renaissance Revival style, imitating great buildings in Europe including the Paris Opera and St. Peter's Basilica in Rome.

On October 4, 1906, President Theodore Roosevelt dedicated the building with the words, "It is the handsomest building I've ever seen." Although Huston had succeeded in creating the building of his dreams, the architect later went to prison, convicted of fraud in the building's financing and construction.

The building's five-story exterior is faced with Vermont granite, and the roof is of green-glazed tile. Four pairs of Corinthian columns grace the entry. The dome, rising 272 feet above the ground, features 48 "bull's-eye" portholes. At its peak is the female figure *Commonwealth* (sometimes called "Miss Penn")—17 feet 8 inches tall.

The rotunda's Carrara marble staircase was inspired by the staircase at the Paris Opera. At the bottom stand "Angels of Light" holding aloft illuminated crystal globes. The great rooms—the Hall of the House is the largest—feature differing Renaissance designs: Italian in the Hall of the House, French in the Senate, English in the Governor's Reception Room. Interspersed throughout the main floor are numerous mosaics representing scenes and artifacts from Pennsylvania history, symbols, insects, and animals. Medallions in the rotunda by Edwin Austin Abbey (1852–1911) describe the four "forces of civilization": *Art, Law, Religion*, and *Science*.

The Senate Chamber walls are lined with green Connamara marble imported from Ireland.

The Hall of the House is dominated by five murals by Edwin Austin Abbey, and 210 varnished mahogany desks. On

session days, the chamber is the busy workshop of 203 legislators (the second largest body after New Hampshire's 400), plus their clerks, pages, and staff assistants. The giant mural behind the House Speaker's podium is Abbey's *The Apotheosis of Pennsylvania*, depicting fifty of the state's historical figures, with Benjamin Franklin and Robert Morris flanking William Penn at the center.

Rhode Island, one of the original thirteen colonies, was settled in 1636 when Roger Williams and a small band of followers left what they viewed as overly repressive Massachusetts to seek freedom of worship.

A series of towns and buildings had served as the center of government (Newport and Providence were once co-capitals) when, in the 1890s, the legislature commissioned construction of a new capitol, to be located on Smith Hill, now Constitution Hill, in Providence. The Rhode Island State House was designed by the New York architectural firm of McKim, Mead, and White (who had recently designed the Boston Public Library). Construction began in 1895, and the cornerstone ceremony, attended by President Grover Cleveland, was held on October 15, 1896. The 235-foot-high building was declared completed on June 11, 1904.

Built of white Georgia marble, the State House is in the usual form for bicameral legislative buildings: a large central dome flanked by two wings. Carved in the marble over the pillared porticos are quotations and historical chronologies of Rhode Island. At the top of the 235-foot-high dome is the bronze statue *Independent Man*. One story is that people wanted a statue of Roger Williams atop the State House, but nobody knew what Roger Williams looked like. So the 14-foot-tall *Inde-*

*pendent Man* has become the symbol of Rhode Island's spirit, freedom, and tolerance.

In the center of the 50-foot-wide rotunda, under the marble dome, is a brass replica of the state seal including an anchor and the word Hope. Only Minnesota's capitol has a larger dome. Inside the dome are murals painted by Giorgio DeFelice depicting *Commerce, Education, Justice*, and *Literature*. The rotunda also features a central chandelier, as well as a mural by James A. King showing Roger Williams leading the colonization of Providence Plantations.

The wings contain the legislative chambers. The Senate Chamber includes the seals of the thirteen original colonies in the arch over the rostrum, with Rhode Island's in the center.

In addition to the House and Senate chambers, the main floor contains the State House Library and the

Only two buildings in the world have larger self-supporting marble domes than Rhode Island's State House: Saint Peter's Basilica in Rome and the Taj Mahal in India.

State Reception Room, the most lavish of the public rooms. Decorated in Louis XIV style, with marble pilasters lining the walls, the room contains an iconic portrait of George Washington by Gilbert Stuart, a Rhode Island native.

"To hold forth a lively experiment that a most flourishing civil state may stand and best be maintained with full liberty in religious concernments."

*Inscription on the south portico*

COLUMBIA SOUTH CAROLINA

South Carolina became the eighth state to ratify the United States Constitution in 1788, and, in 1790, moved its seat of government from Charleston to the new city of Columbia in the state's midlands.

Seventy years later, South Carolina would be the first state to secede from the Union when it ratified the Ordinance of Secession on December 20, 1860. The first shots of the Civil War were fired in Charleston harbor on April 12, 1861. Not only did South Carolina fight on the losing side, but the state suffered disproportionately when Union Army General William Tecumseh Sherman's march through the state left a trail of absolute devastation.

Work on South Carolina's State House began on December 15, 1851, but was suspended when Sherman's army destroyed Columbia on February 17, 1865. Because of the costs of recovering from the war, construction stalled for some thirty years. In 1900, the present dome and north and south porticos were completed. The design and construction were both controversial. A joint legislative committee criticized South Carolina's new 180-foot-tall dome: "No uglier creation could be devised," it lamented, "and it is nothing short of a miserable fraud." The building was to the point where it could be called finished in 1907, and it was completely renovated between 1995 and 1998.

The building is in the Italian Renaissance style. Granite for the structure came mostly from the Granby quarry, located about two miles to the south. Each of the Corinthian columns that support the porticos is carved from a single piece of stone.

The interior design is unique. Every rectangular building with a round dome has to have a transition from rectangular to round. Most domed capitols carry the roundness of the dome down into a rotunda. South Carolina is different, maintaining the rectangular shape all the way up through the top floor, with a huge rectangular reception room between the legislative chambers. Some thirty feet up, in the center of the reception room ceiling, the dome begins.

A statue in the lobby and a portrait in the Senate chamber honor South Carolinian John C. Calhoun (1782–1850), U.S. Senator, Secretary of War, Secretary of State, and Vice President, best known as a proponent of slavery and extreme advocate of state's rights.

Outside the south portico, a prominent statue honors J. Strom Thurmond (1902–2003), member of the South Carolina senate (1933–1938) third-party Presidential candidate (1948), Governor of South Carolina (1947–1951), and U.S. Senator—who represented South Carolina in Washington D.C. for fifty years, from 1954 until 2003. The statue greeting visitors in front of the capitol is of George Washington. Magnolia and palmetto trees give the grounds a tropical atmosphere.

Settlers began flooding into the Dakota Territory in 1878, following the discovery of gold in the Black Hills, the defeat of the Sioux, and the death of the great Sioux leader Crazy Horse.

With population shifting north, the territorial capital moved from Yankton to Bismarck (now the capital of North Dakota), spurring the effort to make South Dakota an independent state. Congress agreed, President Grover Cleveland signed the bill, and South Dakota became the 40th state, on November 2, 1889. Many towns campaigned to be designated the permanent capital of the new state. Pierre won, largely because of its central location.

Following one last dispute, when the state almost moved its capital to Mitchell, construction of South Dakota's capitol building in Pierre began in 1905, and the completed building was dedicated on June 30, 1910. A modified version of the Montana state capitol in Helena, it was designed and built by Minneapolis architects C. E. Bell and M. S. Detwiler. The structure is 161 feet tall and features carved woodwork and marble, specially cast brass, hand-laid mosaics, native field stone, Indiana limestone, and Vermont and Italian marble. The dome is solid copper. Ceilings, wall decoration, color schemes, window treatments, and carpets throughout the building were restored in time for the state's centennial in 1989.

The height of the rotunda, from the floor to the top-center black circle, is 96 feet. The capitol's classical architecture contains much symbolism. Under Victorian leaded stained glass atop the rotunda are 16 oval alcove openings, each centered on a painting of the *Tree of Life*. In the corner alcoves, four bronze sculptures—representing *Wisdom, Vision, Courage*, and *Integrity*—date from South Dakota's centennial year. The rotunda floor is a combination of American-laid prism glass and Italian Terrazzo tile, with a small gold triangle at the exact center. The reinforced concrete columns are surfaced with *scagliola* made of milk, ink, yarn, and marble dust.

The grand staircase was constructed of white cloud marble from Tennessee and Vermont. (One of the spindles was installed upside down.)

In the legislative chambers, marble water fountains are carved with seashells and pasque flowers (*Pulsatilla hirsutissima*), the South Dakota state flower. Above the flowers, acanthus leaves symbolize wisdom. The drinking fountains seem too high, because originally there were no fountains, just high basins filled with water. Small tin cups sat on the ledge and people who wanted drinks shared the cups. Plumbing was added later.

Tennessee is the sixteenth state, admitted in 1796. The state capitol, located on a prominent hill in downtown Nashville, was completed in 1859.

The building was designed in the Greek Revival style by William Strickland, who also supervised construction until his unexpected death in 1854. According to his wishes, he was buried in the walls of the capitol; his tomb can be seen at the northeast corner of the building near the entrance.

Strickland's design resembles a Greek temple with a tower. The exterior and interior walls are massive Bigby limestone blocks, quarried nearby, shaped, and transported to the site by convicts and slaves. The building consists of a Doric basement, four Ionic porticos resembling the Erechtheum in Athens, two of eight columns and two of six columns—each column four feet in diameter—surmounted by the Corinthian tower in the center of the roof. The lantern imitates the Choragic Monument of Lysicrates near the Acropolis in Athens. The whole height is 170 feet. Inside, Strickland made extensive use of cast iron, a futuristic building material for the time.

Originally, the interior included space on the ground floor for the governor's office, the state archives, offices of the secretary of state, the treasurer, and the register of land, as well as the Tennessee Supreme Court, a federal district court, and the Repository of Official Weights and Measures. The main floor contained the assembly halls for the House of Representatives and the Senate, legislative committee rooms, and the state library, which

is one of the finest rooms in the capitol, featuring cast-iron stacks, galleries, and a cast-iron spiral staircase connecting the various levels. The capitol features numerous works of art, historical murals, frescoes, portraits, and massive chandeliers.

The grounds feature three United States Presidents from Tennessee: a dominating equestrian statue of Andrew Jackson, a statue of Andrew Johnson, and the tomb of James K. Polk.

# AUSTIN **Texas**

The Texas state capitol was designed by Elijah E. Myers—architect of the Michigan and Colorado capitols—who won the nationwide design competition in 1881. Contractors were given three million acres in the Texas Panhandle in exchange for constructing the capitol. This acreage would become the famous XIT Ranch.

Completed in 1888 and dedicated on April 21 of that year, the capitol is Renaissance Revival in style, based on the architecture of fifteenth-century Italy, characterized by classical orders, round arches, and symmetry. The exterior is "sunset red" granite, quarried 50 miles away in Marble Falls, Texas. The state gave the contractor 1,000 convicts to quarry the stone. When the local granite cutter's union objected to the use of convicts, the contractor imported experienced stonecutters from Scotland. The foundation is limestone with structural support provided by masonry walls and cast-iron columns and beams.

The people of Texas boast that their capitol is the largest of all state capitols. More than 310 feet in height, it is seven feet taller than the national Capitol in Washington, D.C. Atop the dome is the statue *Goddess of Liberty*.

Inside, the rotunda and the five levels of public corridors that surround it are lined with elaborate classical ornamentation—carved woodwork, plaster moldings, cast-iron columns, stairways, and acid-etched windows and transoms. Carved door frames have bronze hinges inscribed with the words "Texas Capitol," and the hinges and other hardware are incised with geometric and stylized floral motifs. The decorative style reflects the fashion of the late 1880s, which was moving away from the Renaissance Revival style found in the building's interior architecture toward simpler decoration known as Modern Gothic.

Legislative chambers are the symbolic heart of a capitol; the House Chamber is the largest room in the Texas capitol (see p. 107).

An underground north extension, completed in 1995, doubled the capitol's square footage. In the late 1990s the capitol and grounds were comprehensively restored and renovated. The nearby General Land Office Building, completed in 1858, now serves as the capitol's Visitor Center, with exhibits on Texas history and the capitol, maps, travel information, and a gift shop.

When Utah became a state, on January 4, 1896, the capital was the central Utah town of Fillmore. With the state's population centering just east of the Great Salt Lake, however, the capital was soon changed to Salt Lake City.

Legislators chose Richard Kletting's "simple, dramatic, and straightforward" Renaissance Revival plan for a 286-foot tall statehouse. Construction on the building, featuring granite from nearby Little Cottonwood Canyon, began December 26, 1912, and the building was dedicated on October 9, 1916. Like most Classical Revival architecture, Kletting's design for Utah is symmetrical in its exterior elevations, stately and formal in its expression, and reliant on a diverse classical decorative expression taken from Greek, Roman, and Renaissance sources. The dome has been called "Walterized Wren" because it bears a strong resemblance to the dome of the U.S. Capitol designed by Thomas U. Walter, which in turn was based on Christopher Wren's design for St. Paul's Cathedral in London

Utah's capitol is on a low hill overlooking downtown Salt Lake City (see p. 106), surrounded by 40 acres of sculpted lawns, trees, flowerbeds, and shrubs. There are 52 Corinthian columns. The dome is covered with Utah copper. Throughout the grounds, on the building itself, and within the capitol's interior are countless representations of beehives, Utah's state symbol, representing industry and cooperation.

Inside, the two wings are lined with marble Ionic columns. The second level houses the offices of the executive branch including the governor and the State Reception Room (Gold Room). On the third level, the House of Representatives is to the west, the Senate to the north, and the Supreme Court to the east. In the center is the rotunda, rising 165 feet above the main floor. The ceiling of the rotunda is painted with clouds and seagulls, the state bird. Twelve paintings lining the rotunda depict scenes from the early history of the state and its settling. Statues in the rotunda include likenesses of Brigham Young and Philo T. Farnsworth, a principal inventor of television.

The lunettes on each end of the Great Hall feature giant murals painted in 1917 by Gerald Hale and Gilbert White. The painting on the west illustrates the Salt Lake valley as it appeared when the Mormon pioneers first saw it on July 24, 1847. The east mural, *Reclaiming the Desert by Irrigation*, depicts the valley one year later, after crops had been planted and irrigated. Several additional murals were the result of the Works Progress Administration (WPA), including depictions of John C. Fremont's first sighting of the Great Salt Lake in 1843 and the "seagulls miracle" of 1848, when seagulls consumed insects that had been destroying the first settlers' crops.

The Republic of Vermont was founded in 1777, during the early years of the Revolutionary War, over the continuing opposition of the authorities in New York. Vermont's 1777 Declaration of Rights became the first American constitution to abolish slavery. From its founding in 1787 through 1807, Vermont's legislature, the General Assembly, met 46 times in 14 different towns. Vermont finally won its independence and was the first state added to the original thirteen, on March 4, 1791.

In 1805, the General Assembly chose Montpelier for the state's permanent capital, if the town would donate land and have a capitol building ready by 1808. The first statehouse deteriorated rapidly, however, and was replaced thirty years later by a classically inspired building of granite (obtained at the Barre quarries some ten miles away) built into the hillside of what is now known as Hubbard Park. A fire destroyed most of that building in January 1857, and the present capitol, incorporating the earlier building's front porch and portico, built in the Renaissance Revival style, and dedicated in 1859, is known as the Vermont State House. On the front porch stands a statue of Revolutionary War hero Ethan Allen, fabled leader of the Green Mountain Boys. Behind the building, additions date from 1888, 1900, and 1987.

The 57-foot-high dome is an exterior feature only, with no rotunda or other interior expression, due to "circumstances during construction." Atop the dome is the 14-foot sculpture *Ceres, Goddess of Agriculture*.

The interior is finished with finely crafted hardwood trim, elliptical staircases, and Vermont marble floors—white marble from Danby, black marble from Isle La Motte in Lake Champlain. The chandeliers and sconces were designed and manufactured in Philadelphia for installation with the first furnishings in 1859. In the ceiling are ornamental plasterworks, Renaissance designs cast in molds prior to installation. First-floor portraits include the two U.S. presidents who were born in Vermont, Chester A. Arthur and Calvin Coolidge.

The House Chamber is home to the 150-member House of Representatives. The chandelier is an unusual designed-for-gas fixture that includes allegorical figures of *Commerce*, *Prudence*, *Eloquence*, and *Science*. In the more intimate Senate Chamber are desks for 30 members. The Senate's chandelier was refurbished and reinstalled in 1981, having gone missing for 65 years.

The Governor's Office in the State House is used for ceremonial occasions and whenever the General Assembly is in session.

RICHMOND VIRGINIA

Virginians are proud to say their legislature started meeting in Jamestown in 1619, a year before the Pilgrims arrived in what would become Massachusetts. (The colonial relationship between Massachusetts and Virginia was always one of both rivalry and partnership.) The Virginia legislature met in Jamestown and then Williamsburg before moving to Richmond in 1780. Thomas Jefferson was asked to design the capitol building, to be built atop Richmond's Shockoe Hill, while he was ambassador to France, in 1785.

In contemplating the design for Virginia's capitol, Jefferson was inspired by classical Roman temples, especially the Maison Carrée in Nîmes, France (then nearly 1800 years old). The cornerstone was laid on August 16, 1785, while Jefferson was still in France. The unfinished building was occupied in October, 1788, and the dome was installed three years later. Landscaping of the grounds, the twelve-acre Capitol Square, was done in 1816. The George Washington monument, northeast of the building, was competed in 1869. The following year, the courtroom floor above the old House of Delegates Hall collapsed, killing 62 and injuring more than 200. Wings for new House and Senate Chambers, imitating Jefferson's original design, were completed in 1906. Construction of an underground extension—including meeting rooms, offices, and exhibition space—leading up into the historic capitol, was completed in 2007.

Only the Maryland State House (completed in 1788) is older than Virginia's capitol, although New Hampshire claims the distinction of having the oldest legislative chambers still in use (since 1819). Jefferson's design became the standard for classically designed state capitols around the country. (Alaska's capitol, for example, originally a warehouse, was made to look like a state capitol by merely adding four columns supporting a shallow portico out front, see p. 117.) The Virginia capitol is made of brick covered with stucco. The six columns supporting the south (front) portico contain their original pine-tree center posts. Limestone floors and walls are marked with fossils of snails and other shells. Because Jefferson wanted the appearance of a classical temple, the top of the dome, 57 feet above the floor, is not visible from outside.

Inside and under the dome, the rotunda boasts Jean-Antoine Houdon's marble statue of George Washington, done in France from detailed measurements and sketches made by the artist in 1785, while Washington was living at Mount Vernon. At six feet two inches, the statue is considered to be a perfect likeness. Also surrounding the main-floor rotunda are sculptures of eight Virginia-born presidents, plus the Marquis de Lafayette.

The old House of Delegates Hall—now a museum—was the scene of Aaron Burr's treason trial in 1807, as well as the fatal collapse in 1870.

On March 2, 1853, Congress designated the part of the Oregon Territory north of the Columbia River as a new territory, naming it Washington in honor the "Father of the Country." Congress approved Washington statehood on the anniversary of George Washington's birthday in 1889, and Washington became the forty-second state on November 11 of that year, the only state in the Union named for a president.

Olympia, which had been the territorial and state capital since 1853, had to fight off factions promoting Vancouver, Ellensburg, North Yakima, and Seattle prior to a 1911 design competition for the new capitol.

Washington State's main capitol building is known as the Legislative Building. It is based on the 1911 competition-winning design of New York architects Walter Wilder and Harry White. Wilder and White's design is patterned after Stanford White's design for the Rhode Island statehouse. Other buildings on the campus—the Temple of Justice, the Administration Building, the Insurance Building, and the Governor's Mansion—were included in their design.

The Legislative Building was completed and opened on March 27, 1928. Unhappy over the high cost of the structure, Governor Roland Hartley said at the opening, "Today is an epochal day, but it brings no joy to the heart of the taxpayer. May the new building be a deterrent, rather than an incentive, to future extravagance on the part of those in whose hands the business affairs of the state are entrusted." It was said, however, that Governor Hartley had made sure his own office in the Legislative Building was the most elegantly appointed of all.

Forty-two steps lead up to the building's front door, commemorating Washington as the nation's

forty-second state. Solidly built, the Legislative Building has withstood several earthquakes, including the Nisqually quake of February 28, 2001, thanks to the excellent structural design, superior craftsmanship of the original builders, and seismic upgrades following earthquakes in 1949 and 1965. At 287 feet high, Washington's Legislative Building is said to have the fourth tallest masonry dome in the world, surpassed by only St. Peter's Basilica in Rome (446 feet), St. Paul's Cathedral in London (355.5 feet), and St. Isaac's Cathedral in St. Petersburg (333 feet). Atop the dome is the 47-foot-high *Lantern of Liberty*. Inside the 174-foot-high rotunda, a five-ton Tiffany chandelier, 25 feet long and 8 feet in diameter, sparkling with 236 light bulbs, hangs from a 100-foot chain.

Exterior sandstone is from Pierce County, Washington. Formosa marble in the Senate Chamber is from Germany; Escalette marble in the House Chamber is from France; Bresche marble in the State Reception Room is from Italy; and the gray marble of the main corridors is from Alaska. The landscaping plan, mostly complete by 1930, is the work of the Olmsted Brothers of Brookline, Massachusetts.

On January 3, 1921, fire raced through the old West Virginia capitol building in Charleston, igniting ammunition recently confiscated from coalfield disturbances, destroying the building. Barely six months later, on July 23, 1921, the quickly organized Capitol Building Commission selected New Yorker Cass Gilbert as architect of a new capitol. To his credit were the capitols of Minnesota and Arkansas, plus New York City's Woolworth Building, then the tallest building in the world.

The new site was 16 acres east of downtown along the north bank of the Kanawha River.

The west wing was completed in March 1925, the east wing in December 1927, and the central structure in February 1932.

When construction extended into the Great Depression, state officials became alarmed that plans called for the dome to be covered with gold. Architect Gilbert, however, asserted that gilding would cost less than stone. "If we had built the dome of stone, as in the Arkansas capitol, or of marble, as in the Minnesota capitol or the Rhode Island capitol," he said, "it would have cost five or ten times as much money… the comparatively modest expense for covering it with newly developed material of lead coated with copper and using gilding, has reduced the cost to a minimum… if the bell of the dome were of limestone it would be, in this climate, susceptible to expansion and contraction and the joints would have to be constantly repaired in order to preserve it." Gilbert noted that several public buildings in the country, including state capitols at Boston, Massachusetts, and Trenton, New Jersey, were surmounted by gilded domes. He prevailed.

The main entrance to West Virginia's capitol is on the Kanawha River side, protected by a monumental Corinthian portico approached by broad flights of steps. Under the steps is a private entrance or *porte-cochère*. The main entrance opens into the rotunda under the dome. Floors are inlaid with Italian travertine, with white Vermont marble in the walls and columns. Arches to the east and west open to the legislative foyers; arches to the north and south open to the porticos. Above the undecorated pendentive brackets is more carved marble in the form of a frieze at the dome's base, and further up is a wrought-iron railing.

In the legislative chambers, the Senate's eagles have their wings spread while the House's eagles have closed wings. Above the Supreme Court Chamber is a rectangular panel of stained glass. *Scale and Balance* and *Book of Law*, bronze carvings, frame the skylight.

George Browne Post & Sons designed the Wisconsin capitol. Post was part of the late nineteenth-century architectural movement that pioneered the use of steel to make taller, stronger structures. Constructed between 1906 and 1917, it is the only state capitol built on an isthmus (between Lake Mendota and Lake Monona).

Wisconsin's capitol is 284 feet high from the ground to the top of Daniel Chester French's gilded bronze statue, *Wisconsin*, atop the dome—three feet shorter than the national Capitol in Washington, D.C. In her left hand, *Wisconsin* holds a globe with an eagle perched on it. On top of her helmet is the state animal, a badger.

Beginning in 1937, a huge electric "W" decorated the dome during the college football season. The "W" was twelve feet high and thirteen feet wide, with 250 bright red light bulbs visible from the University of Wisconsin to the west. The lighted sign was removed in 1942, to conserve energy during World War II.

Edwin Blashfield's mural *Resources of Wisconsin* lavishly decorates the ceiling of the rotunda, the only granite dome in the United States. The pendentives, which make the transition from the octagonal rotunda to the circular dome, are decorated with mosaics designed by Kenyon Cox, who also painted murals for the capitols of Iowa and Minnesota.

The state's diverse ethnic heritage is reflected in the architecture, art, and furnishings throughout the capitol, including 43 varieties of stone from around the world, hand-carved furniture, and glass mosaics. Styled after the council chambers of the Doge's Palace in Venice, the walls and ceilings of the Governor's conference room are adorned with historical and allegorical paintings by Hugo Ballin. The room also boasts French walnut furniture and a Wisconsin hardwood floor.

The heritage theme echoes in the chambers of Wisconsin's legislature and high court. The State Supreme Court is decorated in German and Italian styles and features extensive use of marble, as well as four murals by Albert Herter. The Senate Chamber is decorated with French and Italian marble, and is highlighted by a colorful skylight and a Kenyon Cox mural depicting the opening of the Panama Canal. Down the hall, the Assembly Chamber features New York and Italian marble, Wisconsin oak furniture, an Edwin Blashfield mural symbolizing Wisconsin's past, present, and future, and a 36-foot circular skylight of low-tone leaded glass, the largest of the four skylights in the capitol.

Until 1968, lake water was piped throughout the capitol so there was no safe drinking water.

CHEYENNE WYOMING

Carved from sections of the Dakota, Utah, and Idaho territories, Wyoming Territory was created by an Act of Congress on July 25, 1868. The arrival of the Union Pacific Railroad in 1867 had changed Cheyenne from a village to a city, and the seat of the new territorial government was established there in 1869. Talk of statehood began immediately, but steps to statehood did not begin until 1888, when the territorial assembly sent Congress a petition for admission into the Union. President Benjamin Harrison signed Wyoming's statehood bill on July 10, 1890, making Wyoming the forty-fourth of the United States.

Wyoming is sometimes known as the "Equality State" because, beginning with statehood in 1890, Wyoming women were the first in the nation to vote, serve on juries, and hold public office. Wyoming has long been the nation's least populous state, with a current population of a little more than half a million people.

Wyoming's capitol, in Cheyenne, is classical Corinthian architecture reminiscent of the national Capitol in Washington, D.C. It is sometimes said to be a smaller version of the Texas Capitol. David W. Gibbs of Toledo, Ohio, was the architect. The cornerstone was laid on May 18, 1887, while Wyoming was still a territory. Flagstone for the building's foundation was quarried near Fort Collins, Colorado, 45 miles to the south; sandstone used in the upper floors came from Rawlins, Wyoming. Wings on either side were completed in 1890 and two final wings, the House and Senate chambers, were finished in 1917. The peak of the dome is 146 feet high, its base 50 feet in diameter. The dome's 24-carat gold leaf is visible from all roads into Cheyenne. For early twentieth-century travelers, the first view of the capitol eight blocks up Capitol Street from the Union Pacific train station was memorable.

The interior is finished in cherry, oak, and butternut. Murals in the Senate and House chambers, painted by Allen T. True, depict industry, pioneer life, law, and transportation. The ceilings of both legislative chambers are stained glass with the state seal in the center. Displayed prominently in the rotunda is a statue of Chief Washakie of the Shoshone, who died in 1900 and is revered as a particularly enlightened Native American leader.

The capitol grounds include statues of Esther Hobart Morris (first woman to be appointed Justice of the Peace, in 1870), a bison (a symbol of the state), and a dynamic bronco-buster cowboy-on-a-horse known as *The Spirit of Wyoming*.

# Comparing Fifty State Capitols

Each of the fifty state capitols is unique in size, shape, style, building materials, and finish. They resist comparison because they are so different from each other. Nevertheless, many claim superlatives of one sort or another. Here is a collection of some superlatives and comparisons.

In twenty states, the STATE CAPITAL IS ALSO THE STATE'S LARGEST CITY. These are Atlanta, Boston, Boise, Charleston, Cheyenne, Columbia, Columbus, Denver, Des Moines, Hartford, Honolulu, Indianapolis, Jackson, Little Rock, Montgomery, Phoenix, Oklahoma City, Providence, Richmond, and Salt Lake City.

Several capital cities also boast a MAJOR PUBLIC UNIVERSITY, including Ohio State University in Columbus, the University of Texas in Austin, Louisiana State University in Baton Rouge, the University of Wisconsin in Madison, Georgia Tech in Atlanta, the University of Utah in Salt Lake City, the University of Hawaii in Honolulu, Michigan State University in East Lansing, the University of Nebraska in Lincoln, the University of South Carolina in Columbia, the University of Minnesota in Minneapolis-St. Paul, Florida State University in Tallahassee, and North Carolina State University in Raleigh.

Forty-four states have MOVED THEIR STATE CAPITALS AT LEAST ONCE. The six states that have had the same capital city since their creations as colonies, territories, or states are Massachusetts, Nevada, North Dakota, Vermont, Washington, and Wyoming.

Many capitols are ON OR NEAR THE BANKS OF RIVERS, including two on the Mississippi (Minnesota and Louisiana) and two on the Missouri (Missouri and North Dakota).

The SMALLEST CAPITAL CITY is Montpelier, Vermont, population about 8,000. The next smallest state capital is Pierre, South Dakota, with about 13,000 people.

▲ *Bismarck has been the capital of North Dakota since the beginning of its statehood*

◀ *Indianapolis, Indiana is also the state's largest city*

*Salt Lake City, Utah's capital, boasts a major university* ▶

Vermont's State House, dating from 1859, is said to have the OLDEST LEGISLATIVE CHAMBERS in their original condition. Several capitols are older. Maryland and Virginia are the oldest, but their legislatures meet in newer additions. New Hampshire claims to have the oldest capitol, dating from 1819, in which the legislature continues to meet in its original chambers, but those chambers have been enlarged.

**HIGHEST:** New Mexico's capitol is at 7,000 feet above sea level, Wyoming's at about 6,000 feet. Colorado's, famously, is one mile high, 5,280 feet, so marked on the front steps.

**TALLEST:** Louisiana has the tallest capitol (750 feet), with Nebraska next (733 feet). Illinois is highest among the domed capitols (405 feet); Texas, at 310 feet, is seven feet higher than the national Capitol.

**BIGGEST:** Many capitols have additions and underground connections to nearby buildings, making it difficult to determine their total size, but it would be difficult to beat Texas under any circumstance. The Texas House of Representatives, 95 by 137 feet, is the biggest of the 99 legislative chambers. State capitols with MAJOR UNDERGROUND ADDITIONS or elegant UNDERGROUND CONNECTIONS with adjacent buildings include Connecticut, Louisiana, Maine, New Mexico, Tennessee, Texas, and Virginia.

▲ *Colorado's capitol has "mile high" markers on its front steps*

▲ *Louisiana has the tallest capitol*

◀ *New Hampshire has the oldest capitol in which the legislature continues to meet in its original chambers*

*The Texas House of Representatives has the largest legislative chamber* ▶

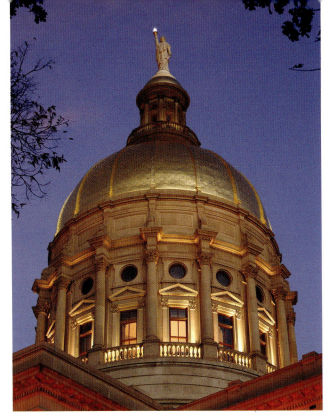

▲ *Georgia's capitol dome is covered in gold*

Ten capitols have **GOLD-COVERED DOMES**: Colorado, Connecticut, Georgia, Iowa, Massachusetts, New Hampshire (cupola), New Jersey, Vermont, West Virginia, and Wyoming.

Eleven capitols are **WITHOUT DOMES**: Alaska, Delaware (cupola), Hawaii, Louisiana, Nevada (cupola), New Hampshire (cupola), New Mexico, New York, North Dakota, Tennessee (cupola), and Virginia.

Five capitols are **WITHOUT ROTUNDAS**: Alaska, Delaware, Nevada, New York, and Vermont.

Only two capitols have been **INTENTIONALLY REPLACED** and then dismantled: New York's in 1883 and Idaho's in 1919. Many capitol buildings were replaced after they were destroyed or heavily damaged by fire. Many predecessor buildings, as in Florida, Illinois, and Louisiana, live on as museums.

There are many examples of **FAMOUS ARTWORKS** in state capitols: N.C. Wyeth's *Battle of Westport* and *Battle of Wilson's Creek* and Thomas Hart Benton's *Social History of the State of Missouri* in the Missouri capitol; Charles M. Russell's *Lewis and Clark Meet the Flatheads at Ross Hole* in the Montana capitol; John Steuart Curry's *Tragic Prelude* in the Kansas capitol (see p. 37); Antonio Canova's sculpture of George Washington in the North Carolina capitol; and Edwin Austin Abbey's *Apotheosis of Pennsylvania and Penn's Treaty with the Indians* in the Pennsylvania capitol. The New Mexico capitol's collection of art is particularly rich and varied.

Washington's solar array, 144 solar panels atop the fifth-floor roof, is said to be the **LARGEST ARRAY OF SOLAR PANELS ON A CAPITOL** in the United States.

Three capitols uniquely **REPRESENT THEIR STATES' WAYS OF LIFE**. New Mexico's capitol, with its **SYMBOLIC ZIA-SHAPE**, is loaded with New Mexican artwork. Oklahoma's capitol boasts an **ACTIVE OIL WELL** out front and vivid Oklahoma **LANDSCAPE ART AND STATUARY** inside. Hawaii's capitol is **SYMBOLIC OF A VOLCANO**, open to tropical breezes and the ever-changing sky.

▼ *New York's capitol has no dome*

▼ *Idaho intentionally replaced its capitol*

▲ *North Carolina's capitol has the sculpture* George Washington *by Antonio Canova*

▲ *The Zia, symbolic of New Mexico, shapes the state's Capitol in Santa Fe*

▲ *Looking up into the "dome" in Honolulu, Hawaii*

*Montana's capitol features the Charles M. Russell mural* Lewis and Clark Meet the Flatheads at Ross's Hole ▼

*Oil well Petunia #1 in front of the Oklahoma capitol* ▶

# Glossary: Architectural Detail and Lexicon

**Arch:** curved, pointed, or flat structure, typically of masonry, forming the upper edge of an open space and supporting the weight above it, as in a bridge or doorway.

**Art Deco:** a style of design at its most popular in the 1930s marked by long, thin forms, curving surfaces, and geometric designs thought to express the sleekness of the machine age.

**Balcony:** platform that projects from the wall of a building, enclosed by a parapet or railing.

▼ *Balcony, Maine*

▲ *Arch, Minnesota*

▼ *Art Deco, Legislative Hall, North Dakota*

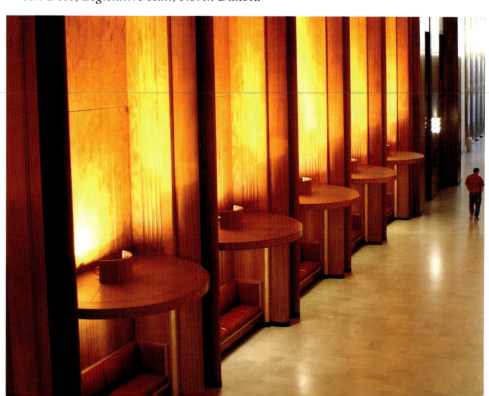

**Balustrade:** row of balusters (upright supports), typically the supporting posts of an ornate handrail.

**Bar:** railing in legislative chamber that separates the general public and staff from the part of the room occupied by legislators; used to bar entry to non-authorized persons and to bar legislators from leaving during a call of the House or Senate.

**Belvedere:** small pavilion or tower on top of a building commanding a wide view.

**Capital:** city that is the seat of government of a state. Also, the top-most feature of a column.

**Capitol:** building recognized as, or symbolic of, the center of state government, known in some states at the "Statehouse" or "State House".

**Chamber:** large meeting room for legislative bodies.

**Clerestory:** high wall with a narrow band of windows along the top.

**Classical:** replication of ancient Greek or Roman architecture.

▲ *Belvedere, Iowa*

▼ *Bar, Senate Chamber, South Carolina*

▼ *Ballustrade, Michigan*

**Column:** narrow, vertical weight-carrying architectural member, circular in cross section, consisting of a base, shaft, and capital (top). Three typical column capital styles are:

- **Doric:** simple, plain
- **Ionic:** features volutes (rolls)
- **Corinthian:** elaborately foliated

**Cornerstone:** large building block, often ceremonially placed as part of a building's foundation or outer wall, symbolic of its construction.

**Cupola:** small, dome-shaped ornamental structure placed on top of a roof.

▲ *Cupola, New Hampshire*

▼ *Ionic columns, Wisconsin*     ▼ *Doric columns, Ohio*     ▼ *Corinthian columns, Utah*

▲ *Dome, Rhode Island*

**Dais:** raised platform at the front of a meeting room, usually reserved for the presiding officer.

**Dome:** large hemispherical vault over a circular opening.

**Fascia:** horizontal band or board, often used to conceal the ends of rafters.

**Filigree:** intricate, delicate, fanciful ornamentation.

**Fossil:** recognizable remnant of an organism from a past geologic age, such as a skeleton or leaf imprint, embedded and preserved in rock.

▲ *Filigree, Tennessee*

▼ *Dais, Senate Chamber, New Jersey*

▼ *Fossils, Virginia*

**Frieze:** horizontal band above a doorway or window, often decorated with carvings or other designs.

**Gallery:** originally the name for a narrow balcony or platform running the length of a wall, now the term is used to mean the public seating and viewing area above or to the side of a legislative chamber.

**Gothic:** a style of late mediaeval architecture characterized by slender piers, counterbalancing buttresses, vaulting, and pointed arches.

**Grand Staircase:** large set of stairs with supporting framework and balusters, often designed as the centerpiece of a large space, a powerful architectural element.

**Granite:** hard igneous crystalline rock composed of coarse-grained feldspar, mica, and quartz, usually grey or dark red, capable of taking a high polish.

▲ *Frieze detail, Illinois*

▲ *Gothic detail, Connecticut*

▼ *Grand staircase, Colorado*

▼ *Gallery overlooking House Chamber, New Mexico*

▲ Lantern atop the dome, Missouri

▲ Lunette, Oklahoma

▲ Pediment, Florida

▼ Marble, West Virginia

▼ Niche, South Dakota

**Lantern:** tower or small turret with openings for light and air, crowning a dome.

**Limestone:** a common sedimentary rock consisting mostly of calcium carbonate, formed millions of years ago by layer upon layer of shells and other remnants in shallow seas, often embedded with fossils.

**Lunette:** crescent-shaped or semicircular area or opening on a wall, frequently above a window or door, sometimes containing a statue or painting.

**Marble:** limestone in a crystalline or granular state, capable of taking a fine polish, used flat as in walls or carved, as in statuary, the most frequently mentioned building material of the state capitols.

**Niche:** a recess in a thick wall.

**Parapet:** low wall on the edge of a balcony, terrace, or roof.

**Pediment:** triangular space above a window, door, or entrance; originally the end of a gable roof, later used decoratively.

**Pendentive:** triangular section of vaulting between the rim of a dome and each adjacent pair of the arches that support it.

**Pier:** vertical, often massive, support structure for a roof, arch, or other enclosed space.

**Pilaster:** rectangular support projecting slightly from a wall resembling a flat column, with a base, a shaft, and a capital.

**Plan:** floor and wall layout of a room or building, as seen from above.

**Portico:** porch leading to a building entrance, with a roof structure over the walkway, supported by columns or enclosed by walls.

▼ *Portico, Vermont*

**Profile:** view of a building from the side or front.

**Rafter:** roof support sloping down from the roof ridge, resting on, and extending over, a wall.

**Renaissance:** a period in Western history, generally the years 1400 to 1600, characterized by the revival of highly symmetrical, carefully proportioned classical architecture.

**Rotunda:** large room or hall, the symbolic center of a building, often covered by a dome.

**Salon (Saloon):** large, high room, frequently with a vaulted ceiling, often used for receptions.

**Sandstone:** sedimentary rock comprising an aggregate of sand-sized fragments of mineral and rock, held together by a mineral cement.

▲ *Skylight, Arizona*

▼ *Rotunda, Oregon*

▲ *Vault, Nebraska*

▲ *Wainscoting, Governor's Reception Room, Arkansas*

**SCAGLIOLA:** imitation marble made with gypsum, glue, pigment, and marble dust.

**SKYLIGHT:** window set into a roof or ceiling to provide extra lighting.

**STATEHOUSE or STATE HOUSE:** capitol building.

**STUCCO:** decorative plasterwork composed of gypsum, lime, and powdered marble. Slow setting, easy to work, it sets very hard.

**SYMMETRY:** exact correspondence of parts on either side of a building.

**TEMPLE FRONT:** entryway in the style of a classical Greek or Roman temple.

**VAULT:** arched structure of stone, brick, or reinforced concrete, forming the supporting structure for a ceiling or roof.

**VESTIBULE:** hall or room between the entrance-door and the main interior of a building.

**WAINSCOTING:** decorative wood paneling covering an interior wall.

▼ *Symmetry, Delaware*

▼ *Temple front, Alaska*

▼ *Scagliola, Idaho*

# Acknowledgments

The author wishes to thank his wife, Joan, his traveling companion, Ruthless, production managers Hinrich and Laurel Muller, editors Jane Stembridge and Michael Smith, and the security and visitors' services personnel in the fifty state capitols for their assistance.

◀ *Kentucky*

# For Further Reference

- *The Capitol Collection* published by DH Tours, LLC (2008), a black-and-white spiral-bound souvenir passport book with space on each capitol's page for an inked stamp mark from each capitol visited.

- *America's Heritage: Capitols of the United States* by Willis J. Ehlert (State House Publishing, Madison, WI, Tenth Edition, 2005, 144 pages), soft-bound, black-and-white photographs.

- *State Houses: America's 50 State Capitol Buildings* by Susan W. Thrane and Tom Patterson (The Boston Mills Press, Erin, Ontario, 2005, 336 pages), lavish color photographs.

- *American Capitols: An Encyclopedia of the State, National and Territorial Capital Edifices of the United States* by Eldon Hauck (McFarland & Company, Inc, Jefferson, NC, 1991 and 2004, 310 pages), illustrations in black and white.

- *State Capitols: Temples of Sovereignty* by Francis Pio Ruggiero (Excelsior Worldwide, Milford, PA, 2002, 670 pages), hard-bound and boxed, color photographs.

- *The American Statehouse: Interpreting Democracy's Temples* by Charles T. Goodsell (University Press of Kansas, Lawrence, KS, 2001, 226 pages), hard-bound academic analysis from Virginia Tech professor Goodsell, black-and-white photographs.

- *The Encyclopedia of State Capitols/Capitals: A Detailed Look at the 50 State Capitol Buildings and the Capital Cities* by Don Severin (Mt. Fanny Publishing, Cove, Oregon, 1999, 322 pages), color illustrations.

- *Domes of America* by Eric Oxendorf and William Seale (Pomegranate Artbooks, San Francisco, CA, 1994, 108 pages), color images "looking up" inside the domes of 43 state capitols.

- *Temples of Democracy: The State Capitols of the U.S.A.* by Henry-Russell Hitchcock and William Seale (Harcourt Brace Jovanovich, New York, 1976, 340 pages), historical illustrations in black and white.

- Numerous books on individual state capitols listed on our website: www.fiftystatecapitols.com.

- If you have questions, comments, corrections, or compliments, please contact the author through: www.fiftystatecapitols.com.

▲ *National Capitol, Washington D.C.*

# Index of Capitols

**Alabama**
Front cover, 2, 4, 5, **6–7**, 71

**Alaska**
3, 5, **8–9**, 97, 108, 117

**Arizona**
3, 5, **10–11**, 41, 59, 71, 116

**Arkansas**
2, 5, **12–13**, 51, 101, 117

**California**
Front cover, 5, **14–15**

**Colorado**
2, 5, **16–17**, 49, 91, 107, 108, 114

**Connecticut**
4, 5, **18–19**, 107, 108, 114

**Delaware**
5, **20–21**, 108, 117

**Florida**
3, 4, 5, **22–23**, 41, 59, 71, 108, 115

**Georgia**
2, 5, **24–25**, 108

**Hawaii**
3, 5, **26–27**, 108, 109

**Idaho**
Front piece, 4, 5, **28–29**, 49, 108, 117

**Illinois**
5, 23, **30–31**, 107, 108, 114

**Indiana**
3, 5, **32–33**, 106

**Iowa**
3, 5, **34–35**, 103, 108, 111

**Kansas**
Front cover, 5, **36–37**, 108

**Kentucky**
2, 3, 5, **38–39**, 118

**Louisiana**
3, 5, 23, 31, **40–41**, 59, 106, 107, 108

**Maine**
2, 4, 5, **42–43**, 107, 110

**Maryland**
1, 2, 5, **44–45**, 63, 97, 107

**Massachusetts**
2, 5, 15, 43, **46–47**, 63, 101, 106, 108

**Michigan**
2, 5, 17, **48–49**, 91, 111,

**Minnesota**
2, 5, 13, **50–51**, 83, 101, 103, 106, 110

**Mississippi**
5, 13, **52–53**, Back cover

**Missouri**
5, **54–55**, 106, 108, 115,

**Montana**
2, 5, **56–57**, 87, 108, 109

**Nebraska**
3, 5, 23, 31, **58–59**, 107, 117

**Nevada**
3, 5, 71, **60–61**, 106, 108

**New Hampshire**
5, **62–63**, 81, 97, 107, 108, 112

**New Jersey**
4, 5, **64–65**, 101, 108, 113

**New Mexico**
3, 4, 5, **66–67**, 107, 108, 109, 114

**New York**
5, **68–69**, 108

**North Carolina**
2, 4, 5, **70–71**, 108, 109

**North Dakota**
3, 5, 41, 59, **72–73**, 106, 108, 110

**Ohio**
Front cover, 2, 5, **74–75**, 112

**Oklahoma**
3, 4, 5, **76–77**, 108, 109, 115

**Oregon**
5, **78–79**, 116

**Pennsylvania**
2, 3, 5, **80–81**, 108

**Rhode Island**
2, 5, **82–83**, 99, 101, 113

**South Carolina**
5, **84–85**, 111, Back cover

**South Dakota**
2, 3, 5, **86–87**, 115

**Tennessee**
5, **88–89**, 107, 108, 113

**Texas**
Front cover, 2, 4, 5, 17, 23, 49, **90–91**, 105, 107

**United States**
2, 15, 51, 59, 91, 93, 103, 105, 107, 120

**Utah**
3, 4, 5, 49, **92–93**, 106, 112

**Vermont**
2, 5, 63, **94–95**, 106, 108, 116

**Virginia**
1, 2, 4, 5, 15, 63, **96–97**, 107, 108, 113

**Washington**
2, 3, 5, **98–99**, 106, 108

**West Virginia**
2, 3, 5, 13, 51, **100–101**, 108, 115

**Wisconsin**
3, 5, **102–103**, 112

**Wyoming**
Table of Contents, 5, **104–105**, 106, 107, 108